VOLUME 6

D1414759

FIRST and SECOND KINGS

Linda B. Hinton

ABINGDON PRESS
Nashville

First and Second Kings

Copyright © 1988 by Graded Press

All rights reserved.

This book is printed on recycled, acid-free paper.

Cokesbury basic Bible commentary.
　　Basic Bible commentary/by Linda B. Hinton . . . [et al.].
　　　　p.　cm.
　　Originally published: Cokesbury basic Bible commentary. Nashville:
　　Graded Press © 1988.
　　ISBN 0-687-02620-2 (pbk.: v. 1: alk. paper)
　　1. Bible—Commentaries.　I. Hinton, Linda B.　II. Title.
　　[BS491.2.C65　1994]
　　220.7—dc20

94-10965
CIP

ISBN 978-0-687-02625-8 (v. 6, 1-2 Kings)
ISBN 0-687-02625-3 (v. 6, 1-2 Kings)
ISBN 0-687-02620-2 (v. 1, Genesis)
ISBN 0-687-02621-0 (v. 2, Exodus–Leviticus)
ISBN 0-687-02622-9 (v. 3, Numbers–Deuteronomy)
ISBN 0-687-02623-7 (v. 4, Joshua–Ruth)
ISBN 0-687-02624-5 (v. 5, 1–2 Samuel)
ISBN 0-687-02626-1 (v. 7, 2 Chronicles)
ISBN 0-687-02627-X (v. 8, Ezra–Esther)
ISBN 0-687-02628-8 (v. 9, Job)
ISBN 0-687-02629-6 (v. 10, Psalms)
ISBN 0-687-02630-X (v. 11, Proverbs–Song of Solomon)
ISBN 0-687-02631-8 (v. 12, Isaiah)
ISBN 0-687-02632-6 (v. 13, Jeremiah–Lamentation)
ISBN 0-687-02633-4 (v. 14, Ezekiel–Daniel)
ISBN 0-687-02634-2 (v. 15, Hosea–Jonah)
ISBN 0-687-02635-0 (v. 16, Micah–Malachi)
ISBN 0-687-02636-9 (v. 17, Matthew)
ISBN 0-687-02637-7 (v. 18, Mark)
ISBN 0-687-02638-5 (v. 19, Luke)
ISBN 0-687-02640-7 (v. 21, Acts)
ISBN 0-687-02642-3 (v. 22, Romans)
ISBN 0-687-02643-1 (v. 23, 1–2 Corinthians)
ISBN 0-687-02644-X (v. 24, Galatians–Ephesians)
ISBN 0-687-02645-8 (v. 25, Philippians–2 Thessalonians)
ISBN 0-687-02646-6 (v. 26, 1 Timothy–Philemon)
ISBN 0-687-02647-4 (v. 27, Hebrews)
ISBN 0-687-02648-2 (v. 28, James–Jude)
ISBN 0-687-02649-0 (v. 29, Revelation)
ISBN 0-687-02650-4 (complete set of 29 vols.)

07 08 09 10—10 9 8 7 6 5

MANUFACTURED IN THE UNITED STATES OF AMERICA

Contents

Outline of 1 and 2 Kings

First Kings

Introduction to Kings

The books of 1 and 2 Kings are part of a history of Israel which begins in Deuteronomy and runs through 2 Kings. The books of Joshua, Judges, 1 and 2 Samuel, and 1 and 2 Kings tell of Israel's settlement in Canaan, of the creation of the state of Israel, of the division of greater Israel into two kingdoms, and of the destruction of these kingdoms by Assyria and Babylon.

Content of First and Second Kings

First and Second Kings were originally one book in Hebrew. The Septuagint (the oldest Greek translation of the Old Testament) put Kings together with Samuel and divided them into "the four books of Reigns/Kingdoms." The books of Samuel and Kings were later separated in both the Hebrew and Christian Bibles. In the Hebrew Bible, First and Second Kings are included in the Former Prophets (Joshua, Judges, First and Second Samuel, and First and Second Kings).

First Kings begins in the last years of King David (962–921 B.C.), and Second Kings ends during the Exile (in approximately 560 B.C.).The content of Kings may be divided into three major sections:

(1) the history of greater Israel from the end of David's reign through Solomon's reign (1 Kings 1–11),

(2) the history of Israel and Judah to the fall of Israel (1 Kings 12–2 Kings 17),

(3) the history of Judah into the Babylonian exile (2 Kings 18–25).

In Kings the word *Israel* has three different meanings. During the reigns of David and Solomon, *Israel* refers to the covenant community (the original twelve tribes) that is united in the nation Israel. After the division of the nation, *Israel* refers to the Northern Kingdom and *Judah* refers to the Southern Kingdom. Even after the division and after the destruction of the Northern Kingdom, however, *Israel* or *the people of Israel* are often used to refer to all the chosen people, both south and north.

The history of the divided kingdoms is organized according to the careers of their kings. The writers give certain information about each king:

Judah	Israel
(1) the king's name; the first year of his reign is coordinated with that of the king of Israel	(1) the king's name; the first year of his reign is coordinated with that of the king of Judah
(2) the king's age, the length of his reign, and his mother's name	(2) the length of his reign and location of his capital
(3) comparison of the king to King David	(3) condemnation of the king's sin and of his leading the people to sin
(4) reference to another book about the kings	(4) reference to another book about the kings
(5) information about the king's death and his successor.	(5) information about the king's death and his successor.

In the books of Kings, each king is judged by the same standard and is either praised or condemned according

FIRST AND SECOND KINGS

to how he lives up to this standard. The historian's standard of judgment is whether the king practices pure worship of God and whether the worship rituals are held in the Jerusalem Temple. Most of the kings are condemned because they allow, or even encourage, the worship of foreign gods. Many of them also build shrines to God away from the Temple, which draws the people away from the Temple for worship.

The Chronology of First and Second Kings

The books of Kings do not give specific dates for the reign of each king. Rather, the reigns are coordinated with one another so that the years of one king are used to establish the years of another (see, for example, 1 Kings 15:25).

This method of dating is not always accurate. Differences exist between these dates and the dates figured by considering only the years of Judean kings or of Israelite kings. In addition, Assyrian and Babylonian documents mention Israelite and Judean kings. Dates from these records do not always match those given in Kings. (For example, from the revolution of Jehu in Israel to the fall of Israel to Assyria is 170 years by the coordinated method, 165 years by the dates for Judean kings, 143 years and 7 months by the dates for Israelite kings, and 121 years according to Assyrian records.)

The coordinated system of dating used in Kings is not completely unreliable, but the dates must be compared to dates given in other historical sources. This is why various Old Testament commentaries do not all give the same dates for the kings of Judah and Israel.

The Writer of First and Second Kings

The books of Kings are the conclusion to the history of the people of Israel which begins in Deuteronomy. The historian(s) who wrote these books are known as the Deuteronomistic historians. They combined parts of many historical records within an interpretive framework to produce the document we have today.

There were possibly two major editions of this document. The first edition may have been written before the death of King Josiah of Judah in 609 B.C. The second edition may have been written around 550 B.C. This was after Judah's defeat by Babylon in 587 B.C. and after many Jews were taken into exile in Babylonia, but it was before the fall of Babylon in 538 B.C. The later writer added material within the earlier structure and perspective. These historians may have been priests or prophets who had access to the records of Israel's history kept in the palace and the Temple. The Jews may have taken some of these records with them when they went into exile.

The viewpoint of Kings is that God acts to bless those who are faithful to the covenant and punish those who disobey the covenant. These actions are in accordance with the law, which is spelled out in Deuteronomy. The writers emphasize that the people of Israel must be faithful to the covenant relationship. In practical terms, this means that the people must not worship other gods nor contaminate their worship of God with foreign practices. All shrines outside of Jerusalem must be destroyed and all worship conducted within the Temple in Jerusalem. In the books of Kings, all the Judean and Israelite kings are strictly judged as to how they lived up to their covenant responsibilities. All idolatry and tolerance of foreign religious influences is condemned.

The Historical Circumstances Behind Kings

The writers of the books of Kings used many reference materials to get information about the history of Israel. Among these materials were official records from the administrations of King David and King Solomon. One of these documents is recorded in 2 Samuel 2:9-20 and 1 Kings 1–2 and is known as the "History of the Throne Succession." This history is believed to be an eyewitness account from the end of David's reign and the beginning of Solomon's reign.

Three historical reference books are mentioned by name in the books of Kings: The book of the Acts of Solomon, The book of the Chronicles of the Kings of Israel, and The book of the Chronicles of the Kings of Judah. The book about Solomon was a collection of stories about Solomon's wisdom and of information from palace and Temple archives. The chronicles of the kings of Israel and of Judah were also official records from the palace archives. These books told of the deeds of each king or queen and of what happened during their rule. The writers of Kings invite their readers to look into these other books for more information on the monarchy and also to confirm what is written in Kings. Unfortunately, these three valuable books are lost to us except for the parts that are preserved in Kings.

The writers of Kings also used stories about the kings, queens, prophets, priests, and others from this time in Israel's history. They included, for example, stories about the ark of the covenant (see 1 Samuel 4:1b–7:2), about the Queen of Sheba (see 1 Kings 13), and about Elijah and Elisha (see 1 Kings 19).

The historians who wrote Deuteronomy, Joshua, Judges, First and Second Samuel, and First and Second Kings used many different resources to produce the document we have today. They used straightforward historical reports as well as history in story form. These historical narratives are told with an awareness of their value as stories as well as an appreciation for the history that they preserve.

Old Testament Historical Narrative

In broad terms, history is defined as what has happened in the past or, in particular, as an account of what has happened in the past. A narrative is a story that, in its simplest form, is a chronological account of more than one past event which also tells of causes and effects. Thus, some narratives can be history that is told as a story. Such stories are common in the Old Testament and are found in the books of First and Second Kings (for example, 1 Kings 19:1-21; 2 Kings 4:8-37).

Old Testament stories are different from other historical narratives, however, because they are sacred stories. These stories are told in the belief that all of life exists because of, and is subject to, God's will. In the Old Testament there is a recognition that some things are holy and others are not, but all life is held to be sacred. Old Testament historical narratives are told within the context of such faith. Because of this faith, Old Testament history is not just a list or report of events. Old Testament history describes events and people and also interprets them according to their causes and effects. God's will is seen as the ultimate source of all causes and effects within human history.

Old Testament historical narrative tells the story of Israel's life as a people who live in relationship to God. The chosen people are the particular subjects of these stories. The broader focus of these stories, however, is the relationship between God and all of creation. The result of this relationship is revelation. God is revealed to humankind. The Old Testament writers do not give us theological lectures about the nature and being of God. Rather, they tell us who God is by telling us how God acts.

The Old Testament writers do not try to convince us to believe their stories by giving us a lot of information about the setting or about the feelings and thoughts of the characters. Most of the time their narratives do not use many details. This reflects the fact that, in many cases, the stories were passed on by word-of-mouth for generations before they were written.

The goal of any narrative is communication. What the writer or speaker knows or sees must be communicated to the reader or listener. The result of narrative is that the readers or listeners see, recognize, and understand something, perhaps something with which they have had no personal experience. The writers of Old Testament stories seek such communication with their readers. Their stories seek to communicate the same basic testimony: History is the will of a just God who knows us and cares about us. The writers want us to understand that our lives are contained in an order that is moving toward God's end.

Old Testament historical narratives witness to the fact that the world and everyone in it belong to God. They ask us to believe that we live in an ordered world which is moving toward a desired goal. The sacred stories of the Old Testament not only offer the pleasure of a well-told story. They teach, encourage, and sustain the community of faith.

Kings of Judah and Israel

Judah	Israel
Rehoboam (922 B.C.)	Jeroboam (922 B.C.)
Abijam (915)	
Asa (913)	
	Nadab (901)
	Baasha (900)
	Elah (877)
	Zimri (876)
	Omri, Tibni (876)
Jehosaphat (873)	
	Ahab (869)
	Ahaziah (850)
	Jehoram (849)
Jehoram (848)	
Ahaziah (842)	Jehu (842)
Athaliah (842)	
Jehoash (837)	
	Jehoahaz (815)
	Jehoash (801)
Amaziah (800)	
	Jeroboam II (786)
Uzziah (783)	
	Zechariah (746)
	Shallum (745)
	Menahem (745)
Jotham (742)	
	Pekahiah (738)
	Pekah (737)
Ahaz (735)	
	Hoshea (732)
Hezekiah (715)	
Manasseh (687)	
Amon (642)	
Josiah (640)	
Jehoahaz (609)	
Jehoiakim (609)	
Jehoiachin (598)	
Zedekiah (597)	

1 Kings 1–2

Introduction to These Chapters

The books of Kings begin during the last years of King David. First Kings 1–2 is part of "The History of the Throne Succession" which is found in 2 Samuel 9–20 and 1 Kings 1–2. The first two chapters of Kings are an introduction to the story of Solomon's reign. First and Second Chronicles also tell about the reigns of David, Solomon, and the other kings of Judah.

David had a long and successful reign. After the death of Saul, the tribes of Israel united under David's leadership and proclaimed him king. They defeated the Philistines, who had been a threat to Israel for many years, and also dealt with their other aggressive neighbors.

David made Jerusalem the political and spiritual center of life in Israel. The ark of the covenant was given an honored place in the new capital.

Under David's military leadership, Israelite territory grew to its greatest dimensions. During this time, the nation of Israel was the dominant power in the ancient Near East.

Though David was undoubtedly a great king and an exceptional man, the end of his life and reign was troubled. As he became older and more feeble the question of who would succeed him as ruler of Israel led to intrigue and violence. This conflict grew out of longstanding disagreements within the nation as well as from the immediate pressures of deciding who would take David's place.

No precedent had been set in Israel for a king's son to succeed him on the throne. Saul and David were both charismatic military heroes. They were leaders among the people who were elected as king through divine benediction and popular acclamation. At the end of David's reign there was still some support for the view that Israel should be led by a charismatic leader whom the Lord would designate as the rightful ruler. In the days of the tribal league, the leaders of Israel were those on whom the people believed the spirit of the Lord rested. A king's son following him in office was more typical of other nations' governments than of Israel. Some Israelites believed that the old, traditional ways were best, and they were distrustful of the strong central power claimed by the king.

There were tensions within the government, the military, the religious establishment, and the royal household. Those who, in the past, had supported Saul against David had little loyalty to David's house despite David's attempts at reconciliation. There was still some resentment among the tribes of Israel at the growing power of the central government and the resulting loss of tribal independence. A proper judicial system had not been established. Because of this there was discontent among the people at the delays in hearing cases and handing down judgments.

The task of holding onto Israel's territory and defending its boundaries placed a great burden on the Israelite military. The fighting force was made up of David's personal professional troops and citizen militiamen from each of the tribes. These militiamen apparently served on a rotating basis with each tribe sending its share of able-bodied fighting men. As the years went by, Israelite citizens became increasingly reluctant to keep up these military duties that took manpower away from the demands of everyday life.

Within the royal household itself there was jealousy and maneuvering for power. David's wife Bathsheba and his two eldest sons, Adonijah and Solomon, were deeply involved in the struggle for the throne. David did not set up an orderly procedure for one of his sons to take his place. He apparently did little to deal with the intrigue even within his own house until the issue of his successor was pressed upon him.

This is the complex and volatile situation with which First Kings opens.

Here is an outline of these chapters.
  I. David's Feeble Condition (1:1-4)
 II. Adonijah Makes His Move (1:5-10)
III. Solomon Becomes King (1:11-40)
 IV. Adonijah Accepts Defeat (41-53)
  V. The Death of David (2:1-12)
 VI. Adonijah, Abiathar, Joab, and Shimei (2:13-46)

David's Feeble Condition (1:1-4)

David is now approximately seventy years old and is in poor health. His attendants try to restore some of his former vitality by bringing a beautiful young woman to serve him. David cannot keep warm even with many covers on him. Nor is he sexually potent even with the warmth and appeal of his lovely handmaiden.

The failure of Abishag to rouse David to new strength intensifies the efforts of those who already want to claim the throne. David's weakened condition and lack of virility may also be seen as a threat to the fertility and prosperity of the people. The idea that the physical welfare of the people was connected to that of the king was common among other peoples of that day. The Israelites may have held such ideas themselves to some extent. If so, then the fact that the king does not have sexual relations with Abishag is an important signal to the rivals for the throne that the time has come to make their move. David can no longer carry out his duties on behalf of Israel.

Adonijah Makes His Move (1:5-10)

Adonijah has reason to believe he can claim the throne. He is David's eldest surviving son, is handsome like his father, and has never caused his father to question his actions or reprimand him. Most people probably realize that only a son of David can hope to hold the loyalty and cooperation of the people of Israel and of the foreign subjects who live within Israel's boundaries. The general expectation is that Adonijah will follow David as king (see, for example, 1 Kings 2:15).

He has supporters among the military and the priesthood. Other powerful people, however, are not with Adonijah (see verse 8), but cast their lot with the younger Solomon. Though Adonijah has fifty soldiers in his personal force, the greater military force is with Solomon, including David's personal bodyguards.

We do not know if Adonijah ever tells David about his desire to be king. Though he may have some suspicion that David favors Solomon over him, David apparently makes no move to stop him when he assembles his force of chariots and soldiers as a sign of his intentions. He then gives a great feast for his supporters at which they hail him as *King Adonijah*. Sharing a meal with someone or accepting someone's hospitality is a symbol of friendship and loyalty.

Solomon Becomes King (1:11-40)

Nathan the prophet realizes that if Adonijah is the new king, then his life as well as Solomon's and all his supporters' lives are in danger. The one who succeeds in gaining the throne will eliminate all of his rivals. Thus, Nathan plots with Bathsheba to manipulate David into declaring Solomon the rightful new king. They realize that, although Adonijah has the prior claim, David's word will carry the most weight among the people.

Verses 28-30: Once the decision is made, David acts with speed and authority despite his ill health. Anyone who makes an oath in God's name is bound to keep it, even if it is rash. Such an oath is both a legal and a sacred obligation, and David knows that his promises concerning Solomon must be carried out.

David's decision is also probably guided by the fact that he knows Solomon is a wise man and will be a capable ruler (see 1 Kings 2:9). It must be said, however, that a strong factor in Solomon's favor is the fact that he is the son of Bathsheba, David's favorite wife.

Verses 32-40: Solomon is to have the honor of riding on the king's mule, the traditional mount for the king and his sons. Ordinary people ride asses. Horses were brought to Israel from Egypt during Solomon's reign, but even then were used for driving rather than for riding.

The *Gihon spring* is in the Kidron Valley and is still accessible today. For many generations it was the principal source of water for Jerusalem.

Solomon's head is anointed with scented olive oil or other perfumed ointment which is kept in the tent of the Lord along with the ark of the covenant. Like Saul (see 1 Samuel 10:1) and David (see 1 Samuel 16:13), Solomon receives his royal authority through this ceremony. He rules as God's anointed servant who exercises power over the people on God's behalf.

The *trumpet* spoken of here is not, strictly speaking, a musical instrument. Rather, it is a ram's horn. These horns are blown as signals of important occasions (for example: coronations, war, peace, the sabbath, and the death of an important person).

Adonijah Accepts Defeat (1:41-53)

Adonijah realizes that his cause is lost and that his life is in danger. He flees to the altar in the tent of the Lord.

This is a traditional place of refuge (see, for example, Exodus 21:12-14). The altar is sacred so a person touching it is not supposed to be killed, but this tradition is not always honored (see, for example, 1 Kings 2:28-34).

Solomon agrees to spare Adonijah as long as he commits no further offense against Solomon and as long as he retires from public life (Go to your *home*).

The Death of David (2:1-12)

David's deathbed charge to Solomon comes in two parts, verses 2-4 and verses 5-9. In the first part, David advises Solomon on how to live in relationship with God. In the second part, he tells Solomon how to deal with David's enemies.

Verses 2-4: David's advice is based on instructions that Moses gave concerning the people of Israel and the rulers of Israel (see Deuteronomy 4:40, 44-45; 17:14-20).

The writers of Kings use these instructions as the standard by which Israel's rulers are to live and rule. They judge every king of Israel and Judah according to this standard. In their judgment, David is a model king according to these requirements, and they compare every Judean king to him (see, for example, 1 Kings 15:3).

God's promise to David about his offspring keeping the throne of Israel was made through the prophet Nathan (see 2 Samuel 7:12-17).

Verses 5-9: David gives Solomon some practical, if harsh, advice on how to secure the throne for David's offspring. He trusts Solomon's abilities to deal with the situation (verse 9) and gives his blessing to what Solomon must do.

Abner and Amasa were under David's protection when Joab killed them (see 2 Samuel 3:26-28; 20:8-10). Because of this, David and his house become bloodguilty. That is, they are responsible for the shedding of innocent blood. This is both a legal and a moral stain on David's house which must be wiped out, though in the past David could not do so himself for political reasons.

In these verses, the belt and the sandals symbolize that which clings closely to a person.

Verse 7: David's friendship with Barzillai (see 2 Samuel 17:27-29; 19:31-39) requires that Solomon show his sons *loyalty* (NRSV) or *kindness* (NIV). The Hebrew word used here for loyalty is often used in the Old Testament to express the faithfulness with which covenant partners keep their responsibilities to one another. This word is sometimes translated as *lovingkindness* or as *mercy* in texts that tell of God's attitude and actions toward the people of Israel and toward the covenant.

Shimei put a curse on David's house which David could not remove (see 2 Samuel 16:5-14; 19:18-23). Solomon must deal with Shimei to remove the burden of this curse from himself.

Verses 10-12: The *city of David* is the old city of Jerusalem which David took from the Jebusites. This part of Jerusalem is located on the hill called the Ophel.

Adonijah, Abiathar, Joab, and Shimei (2:13-46)

Adonijah becomes a threat to Solomon, and Solomon has him killed. He appears to want some of Solomon's royal prerogatives for himself by requesting that Abishag be given him in marriage. Solomon reacts to Adonijah's request by having him killed (verses 12-25). Solomon must have considered Abishag to be a royal concubine or, at least, part of the royal "property" which he inherited from David.

For a man to have sexual intercourse with another man's concubine is viewed as an attempt to take over the latter's authority. In the royal house, such an act is considered rebellion against the king (see 2 Samuel 16:20-22). Israelite tradition also holds that the man who inherits the king's wives and concubines is the new king (see, for example, 2 Samuel 12:7-8).

Solomon cannot have Abiathar killed because he is a priest and his life is not legally Solomon's to take. Abiathar is banished from his duties at the shrine in Jerusalem and is confined to his ancestral home. Verse 27 is an editorial comment which is based on 1 Samuel 2:27-36.

Joab finds no safety at the altar (see above, 1 Kings 1:41-53). His death is of both political and religious advantage to Solomon (verse 33).

Shimei did not side with Adonijah against Solomon, so the king does not execute him at first. Shimei, however, breaks his oath to stay in Jerusalem and pays for it with his life. Thus, Solomon completes David's instructions to him and takes firm control of his kingdom.

§ § § § § § §

The Message of 1 Kings 1–2

The basis for David's instructions to Solomon concerning his kingship (see 1 Kings 2:1-4) is found in Deuteronomy 4:40-45; 17:14-20; and 2 Samuel 7:12-17. According to Deuteronomy, what are the standards for the ideal king?

§ If the king keeps God's statutes and ordinances, the king and the people will prosper in the Promised Land.

§ The king must be a native Israelite.

§ Military alliances, marriage, and the pursuit of riches must be limited because these can lead the king and the people away from God.

§ The king must study the law of Moses.

§ The king must fear God.

§ The king must keep the law and the statutes and ordinances by which the law is applied to daily life.

§ The king must not be proud in relation to the people. Everyone is under the law, including the king.

§ The king is God's servant on behalf of the people.

§ If the king abides by all these standards, he may reign in peace and his descendants will rule after him.

The promises given the king in the Mosaic law are conditional. Peace, stability, and prosperity are related to faithfulness to the covenant requirements. King David applies the conditional aspects of the promises in Deuteronomy to the promises made in 2 Samuel when he speaks to Solomon. In 2 Samuel God promises to punish the king's sins but not to destroy David's dynasty (*house*, 2 Samuel 7:16).

In later years, God's promises concerning the permanent establishment of a king in David's line are taken for granted by kings and people alike while the conditional aspects of the covenant are largely ignored. Solomon himself fails to abide by all the standards set out in Deuteronomy. Old Testament hopes for the restoration and renewal of the people of Israel come to focus on a messiah who is in the line of David or is an ideal king in the tradition of David (see, for example, Micah 5:2-4). Though David's descendants are no longer on the throne of Judah after 587 B.C., David's dynasty is not destroyed. Jesus is born into the family of David to establish an everlasting kingdom.

§ § § § § § §

Introduction to These Chapters

First Kings 3–11 tells of the reign of Solomon. This account is based, in part, on "the Book of the Acts of Solomon" (see 1 Kings 11:41). Chapter 3 introduces the history of Solomon's reign by telling of the divine gift of wisdom by which he governs.

These chapters may be outlined as follows.
I. Solomon Receives Wisdom (3:1-15)
II. Judgment Between Two Mothers (3:16-28)
III. The Organization of Solomon's Kingdom (4:1-34)

Solomon Receives Wisdom (3:1-15)

Solomon's wisdom is unique and is the hallmark of his life as king. The writers of Kings naturally, therefore, begin their history of his reign with how he comes to be so wise.

Verses 1-3: These verses explain why Solomon is sacrificing at Gibeon outside of Jerusalem (verses 4-15). Such an explanation is necessary because the writers of Kings are opposed to any worship outside of the Temple in Jerusalem (see, for example, Deuteronomy 12:1-14).

Solomon has not yet built the Temple in Jerusalem (Chapter 6), his own house (7:1-2), the wall around Jerusalem (9:15), or the house for his Egyptian wife (7:8).

His marriage to an Egyptian princess is a diplomatic alliance with the ruling dynasty in Egypt. The fact that

Solomon is given her hand in marriage is an indication of the power of the kingdom of Israel at this time. Egyptian princesses were not normally married to foreigners.

Verses 4-9: In the Old Testament view, understanding is not something which human beings naturally have. Human understanding can only be a gift from God. In response to God's offer of favor, Solomon confesses his inexperience in leadership and humbles himself before God. He bases his request to God on two facts: (1) God was faithful to the promises made to David (verses 6-7), and (2) Solomon is committed to act as God's servant on behalf of the people of Israel even though he lacks understanding and experience (verses 7-9).

That Solomon speaks of himself as *a little child* does not mean that he is a child in age. This is an expression of his humility and of his awareness of the monumental task before him.

Verses 10-15: Understanding (NRSV; NIV = *discernment*) involves practical judgment rather than theoretical understanding. This ability is a gift from God.

Judgment Between Two Mothers (3:16-28)

The case of the two women both claiming the same child is given as an example of Solomon's skill at exercising judgment. Since there were no witnesses to what happened except the women, this is a particularly difficult case to resolve.

The way Solomon gets the women to reveal the truth shows that his wisdom is not limited to knowing the fine points of the law. He also knows much about human nature.

The Organization of Solomon's Kingdom (4:1-34)

Chapter 4 tells how Solomon's kingdom is organized and further praises his wisdom. Though this chapter pictures Solomon's reign as one of peace and prosperity for Israel, the increasing power and expense of the state brings increasing burdens for the people.

Verses 1-6: These men are Solomon's cabinet-level officials. The *king's friend* (NRSV; NIV = *personal advisor*) is probably the king's trusted counselor or companion.

Forced labor (verse 6) is an Israelite labor force used by Solomon for his building projects. Laborers are required to work only for the duration of a given project and are not permanent state laborers as are foreign slaves. Even so, there is criticism of this practice even as far back as the prophet Samuel, who lists forced labor as one of the dangers of a monarchy (see 1 Samuel 8:11-18).

Verses 7-19: Solomon organizes the country into twelve administrative districts, which sometimes are the same as the old tribal divisions but often are not. Each district has a governor who is responsible to the king. The purpose of this organization is to raise revenues for the state. Each district is responsible for furnishing provisions for Solomon's court for one month out of the year (verse 27). The amount of provisions needed (verses 22, 28) places a great burden on the people.

With this administration Solomon not only brings in revenues but also further consolidates power in his own hands. Tribal loyalties are broken up and weakened. The Canaanites living in Israel are brought more firmly under the power of the state by paying their share of the taxes.

Verses 20-28: These verses praise the prosperity, dominion, and military strength of Israel under Solomon. In the estimation of the writers, the people of Israel enjoy the blessings of fruitfulness promised Abraham (see Genesis 22:15-18). They have good crops and also the peace and security in which to enjoy their bounty.

Some people do enjoy prosperity during this time. The prosperity is not evenly distributed, however, and some people struggle to survive. Until this time Israel had been primarily an agricultural and pastoral society. Under Solomon's ambitious rule the nation becomes increasingly commercial, industrial, and urban. The further integration of the Canaanite population into Israelite life brings different ideas about religion and about class distinctions. The weakening of tribal democracy and the growth of a wealthy commercial class increase the gap between the rich and the poor in Israel. Solomon's court promotes the growth of an aristocratic class who, in some cases, look on the Israelite people as subjects to be used for their personal advantage. Because of this, the seeds of discontent are sown within Israel from the very beginning of Solomon's reign.

Solomon's empire is not without its external conflicts as well, despite the glowing testimony of strength given in verses 21 and 25. In fact, Solomon loses some territory which David had won (see 1 Kings 11:14-25).

Verses 29-34: Solomon's wisdom and fame are proclaimed. The *people* (NRSV; NIV = *men*) *of the east* are wandering Arab tribes to the east of Israel who are famous for their practical wisdom. Egypt, to the west of Israel, was long known as a source of wisdom.

Solomon is wise not only in matters of state but also in composing proverbs and songs. Proverbs are brief, colorful sayings concerning the conduct of everyday life (such as are found in the "Proverbs of Solomon" in Proverbs 10:1-22:16; 25:1–29:27). His songs are probably like the lyrical poems found in The Song of Solomon.

Solomon's wisdom also extends to the natural world. He understands the ways of nature as well as the ways of people.

§ § § § § § §

The Message of 1 Kings 3–4

First Kings 3:12 says that Solomon is given a *wise and discerning mind* (NRSV; NIV = *heart*). According to the Old Testament, what is wisdom?

§ Part of wisdom is understanding, which is practical judgment rather than theoretical understanding.

§ Wisdom is action as well as thought, skill as well as perception.

§ Wisdom comes from a person's heart as well as mind. The heart is the source of a person's character, the wellspring of hopes, fears, attitudes, motives, and beliefs.

§ Wisdom is gained through experience and through study.

§ Fear of God is the beginning of true wisdom (see Proverbs 9:10). Fear of God is reverence and awe for God's holiness and a recognition of one's humbleness in relation to God. Thus a proper appreciation of one's place in the divine order is necessary for wisdom.

§ The human capacity for wisdom and wisdom itself are gifts from God.

§ Wisdom begins with one's relationship to and faith in God.

§ Because wisdom begins with and rests on faith, wisdom has an ethical aspect which includes uprightness and honesty.

§ Wisdom is to be applied in the experience and mastery of life and its problems.

§ § § § § § §

1 Kings 5–8

Introduction to These Chapters

Chapters 5–8 tell about Solomon's alliance with King
Hiram of Tyre and about the building of the Temple and
Solomon's palace (see also 2 Chronicles 2–7).

In addition to his wisdom, Solomon is well known for
the development of commerce in Israel and for the
building of the Temple in Jerusalem. Both of these goals
are achieved, in part, through Solomon's abilities as a
statesman. His foreign policy includes alliances with
other states through marriage with foreign noblewomen
(see, for example, 1 Kings 3:1) and through treaties. One
of the most important treaties is made with the
Phoenician king, Hiram of Tyre.

The Phoenician city-states controlled the Palestinian
coast in what is now Lebanon from Mount Carmel
northward for about 130 miles. They were a great
seafaring trading power. They sold timber from their
mountains, worked bronze, iron, glass, gold, and ivory,
and were famous for dying cloth a prized purple color
with an extract from sea snails. Their trading colonies
eventually extended to the Atlantic coasts of Spain and
Morocco. (See Ezekiel 27 for a description of Tyre's
trading empire from approximately 585 B.C.).

Israel forms the land bridge between Mesopotamia,
Egypt, and Arabia, and thus holds the principal land
trade routes from one to the other. Tyre (and other
Phoenician city-states) controls shipping routes in the

eastern Mediterranean. The combination of these two powers is an advantage to both Solomon and Hiram.

Here is an outline of 1 Kings 5–8.
  I. Agreement Between Solomon and Hiram (5:1-18)
  II. Building the Temple (6:1-38)
  III. Solomon's Palace (7:1-12)
  IV. Temple Furnishings Are Built (7:13-51)
  V. Dedication of the Temple (8:1-66)
    A. The ark and God's glory (8:1-11)
    B. Solomon addresses the people (8:12-21)
    C. Solomon's prayer on behalf of Israel (8:22-53)
    D. Benediction and charge to the people (8:54-61)
    E. Conclusion of the dedication feast (8:62-66)

Agreement Between Solomon and Hiram (5:1-18)

Hiram seeks to continue the friendly relationship begun with Israel during David's reign. Solomon sees an immediate advantage in this because he wants to build a temple but lacks the proper materials and skilled labor to do it.

Verses 3-5: Additional reasons for David's failure to build the temple are given in 2 Samuel 7:1-13 and in 1 Chronicles 22:6-10.

The term *rest* means the possession of God's gifts (the land and its bounty) and the security in which to employ these gifts. Solomon enjoys such rest and freedom from opponents and disasters only in the beginning of his reign, however, before the rebellions and unrest spoken of in 1 Kings 11:14-40.

God's name and face both are signs of God's presence with Israel. In some cases in the Old Testament the Hebrew word for *face* is translated as *presence* (see, for example, Genesis 4:16; Numbers 6:25; Ezekiel 43:7-9). The Temple will be the place where God's special presence will dwell among the people.

Verse 6: The Near East had more abundant forests in

ancient times than it does today, though it has always been a wood-poor region. In ancient times the forests of Lebanon were cut without reservation both by the Phoenicians and by invaders to the area. In 1974 only 400 of the giant cedars remained in Lebanon. In recent years, efforts have been made to replant and replenish forests in some areas of Lebanon and Israel.

Cedar from Lebanon is famous for its resistance to rot and to insects. The wood is also close-grained and well suited for carving.

Verses 7-10: Solomon trades Israel's agricultural products for Hiram's timber. Pressed olive oil is a fine grade of olive oil produced by crushing the olives in a mortar rather than by treading them.

Verses 13-18: Israelites are required to labor for the king three months out of the year, one month in Lebanon and two months on building projects in Israel. This is a severe drain on manpower and a hardship on families. It has been estimated that 30,000 Israelites in Solomon's day are approximately equal to six million Americans in 1960. Such forced labor is deeply resented among the people of Israel.

Building the Temple (6:1-38)

Chapter 6 tells how the Temple is built, including its measurements and the materials and techniques used in its construction.

Verse 1: The information on which the writers base their figure of 480 years from the Exodus to the building of the Temple is not known. Solomon's fourth year as king is approximately 957 B.C. which, according to these figures, would put the Exodus in approximately 1440 B.C. Other historical sources suggest, however, that the Exodus from Egypt came during the reign of Pharaoh Rameses the Great (approximately 1291–1224 B.C.).

It is important to keep in mind that some dates in biblical history are known precisely and some are only approximate. Most ancient documents have been lost or destroyed, so there are often few sources of information other than the Bible for this time in history. This situation is complicated by the fact that ancient systems of dating do not correspond to our present calendar. Also, not all ancient dating systems are alike. Keep this in mind as you study the history of Israel, especially when you find references which give differing dates for the same event.

Verses 2-10: The cubit used in this description of the Temple is probably the royal cubit, approximately twenty-one inches. Thus, the floor is approximately 105 feet long by 35 feet wide. The ceiling is approximately 52.5 feet high. These are interior measurements with the thickness of the walls not specified (the walls are perhaps six cubits thick; see Ezekiel 41:5).

The *vestibule* (NRSV; NIV = *portico*), is the entrance hall, the *nave* (NRSV) is the main *hall* (NIV), and the *sanctuary* is the Holy of Holies in which the ark of the covenant will be kept. This division of the structure into three main rooms is typical of many temples in the ancient Near East.

Side rooms are built around the outside of the building below the high windows in the nave. These rooms probably hold the Temple treasury, which would include religious objects as well as gifts and treasures given to the Temple (as in 1 Kings 7:51).

Verse 7: Undressed stone is used to build the Temple. This reflects the ancient tradition of building altars of undressed stones (see Exodus 20:25; Deuteronomy 27:5-6).

Verses 11-13: God's word to Solomon is based on the promises made to David concerning his offspring and the Temple (see 2 Samuel 7:12-16). Solomon must keep God's law (*commandments*) and obey the rules by which the law is applied to daily life (*statutes* and *ordinances*). If Solomon is true to this responsibility, he and all the people of Israel will be blessed with God's presence.

The promises and responsibilities God gives Solomon

FIRST AND SECOND KINGS

are also based on the covenant relationship established between God and the people of Israel at Sinai (see Deuteronomy 5:1-21; 7:12-16).

Verses 14-22: The interior of the Temple is lined with cedar that is ornately carved (see also verse 29). The palm trees, gourds, and open flowers are common symbols of life and of fertility in the ancient Near East. The cherubim are traditional guardians of sacred places.

In regard to the gold decorations, the word that is translated *overlaid* may instead mean *inlaid.* This would mean that the entire surface of the rooms is not covered with gold but is adorned with gold.

The cedar and gold altar may stand in front of the entrance to the Holy of Holies.

The golden chains may form a veil in front of the Holy of Holies or may pull a veil across the entrance.

Verses 23-30: Likenesses of cherubim guard the ark of the covenant (see Exodus 25:10-22; also Ezekiel 1:4-14 for a description of the cherubim that support God's chariot/throne).

Verses 31-36: The olive tree is very important to life in Israel and is counted among the blessings of the Promised Land (see Deuteronomy 6:11). It provides food, fuel, building material, and medicines.

The *inner court(yard)* is the area in front of the building that is fenced with stone and cedar. In this forecourt stand the great altar and the molten sea.

Solomon's Palace (7:1-12)

These verses describe the palace and administrative buildings that are built just south of the Temple.

The *Palace* (NIV; NRSV = *House*) *of the Forest of Lebanon* gets its name from its cedar pillars and paneling that come from Lebanon. Some of Solomon's treasures are kept here (see 1 Kings 10:17, 21).

The *Hall of Pillars* (NRSV; NIV = *a colonnade*) is probably a waiting room for people seeking entrance to the Throne Room (Hall of Judgment). The Throne Room may be where Solomon hears such cases as that of the two women (see 1 Kings 3:16-28).

These rooms are connected to the king's private apartments, though the exact arrangement is not known.

Temple Furnishings Are Built (7:13-51)

The nation of Israel does not yet have skilled metalworkers, so King Solomon must import an expert from Tyre. The Hebrew word that is here translated *bronze* (verse 14) means both copper and bronze. Bronze is an alloy of copper and tin.

Verses 15-22: Hiram constructs two huge, free-standing *pillars* that are ornately decorated. Their significance is unknown. Judging from the meaning of their names (see the Glossary), they may symbolize both God's strength and support on behalf of the Temple and the people.

Verses 23-26: The *molten sea* (NRSV; NIV = *the sea of cast metal*) is a large tank or basin that is supported by twelve bronze oxen. According to 2 Chronicles 4:6, the water in the basin is for the priests to wash in (as part of their ritual duties). The sea may symbolize life-giving water, or it may symbolize the cosmic waters over which God exerted dominion at Creation (see Genesis 1:1-2, 9-10).

Verses 27-39: The *stands* are bronze wagons on which are mounted the lavers or wash basins. These basins are apparently for ritual washing (see Exodus 30:18-21; 2 Chronicles 4:6).

Verses 48-51: The *golden altar* stands in front of the Holy of Holies and is used to burn incense.

The *bread of the Presence* (also called shewbread) is a continual offering to God (see Leviticus 24:5-9).

The treasures David dedicated are gifts and spoils of war set aside as devoted to God (see 2 Samuel 8:10-12).

Dedication of the Temple (8:1-66)

Chapter 8 tells about the ark of the covenant and the dedication of the Temple.

The Ark and God's Glory (8:1-11)

Verses 1-5: Leaders from three areas of Israelite life gather to bring the ark into the Temple: the king, the tribal and family leaders, and the priests. The ark, the tent sanctuary, and the vessels for worship are brought into the Temple from the city of Jerusalem, which is south of the Temple (see 2 Samuel 6:12-15).

Ethanim, the seventh month in the Hebrew calendar, is mid-September to mid-October. This is the time for the feast of Booths (Tabernacles), which comes at the end of the agricultural year (see Leviticus 23:33-36). This feast is held in remembrance of Israel's time of wandering in the wilderness and in renewal of Israel's covenant responsibilities.

Verses 6-11: The tent of meeting is replaced by the Temple as the home of the ark and as the site of God's special presence with the people. The Israelites exchange the tent, part of their lives as wanderers, for the Temple, a sign that they are settled in the Promised Land.

The *poles* are used to carry the ark (see Exodus 25:10-22).

The *cloud* is a sign of God's presence (see also Exodus 14:19-20; 33:9; 40:34-38) that enters the Temple after the ark is placed there. The priests cannot perform their duties in the Temple because they are overwhelmed by the presence of God's glory. This glory is a manifestation of God's complete power and holiness.

Solomon Addresses the People (8:12-21)

Verses 12-13: Solomon opens his address to the people with a poem that speaks of the power and mystery of God. The Lord of Creation is not to be found in the most brilliant star in our sky; rather, God has chosen to dwell among the people in darkness (or *in a dark cloud*). Solomon's Temple will be a place in which God's presence, though hidden, may dwell among the people.

Verses 14-21: Solomon tells the people why the Temple

was built by summarizing the promises God made to King David through the prophet Nathan (see 2 Samuel 7:4-17). He then connects the Temple with key events in Israel's life as a nation: the giving of the law, the establishment of the covenant, and the Exodus. The Temple, as the place of God's presence in Israel, becomes another of God's gracious and saving acts on behalf of God's people.

Solomon's Prayer on Behalf of Israel (8:22-53)

Solomon praises God's infinite greatness, power, and faithfulness. He speaks of many difficult situations in which the people of Israel have found and will find themselves: war, pestilence, famine, exile, and conflict among themselves. He asks God's mercy and help in their times of need.

Solomon's petitions are based on God's past acts of salvation for Israel (the Exodus, the covenant, and the giving of the land) and on God's promises concerning the lineage of David. A special relationship exists between God and Israel. In this relationship, God is both Israel's gracious redeemer and Israel's judge. Israel is God's inheritance or possession, for the people of Israel are set aside out of all the peoples of the earth as God's very own. The people must live in wholehearted devotion to God. When they fail they must acknowledge their sin and seek God's mercy in true repentance.

Verse 27: The phrase referring to heaven and then the highest heaven literally means *the heaven of heavens*. This type of phrase is used in Hebrew to indicate something that is superior to everything of its kind.

Verses 29-30: A person's *eye* is a bridge between the outer world and his or her consciousness. God's eyes symbolize God's awareness of and attention to the Temple and its worshipers.

Just as God's attention is asked toward the Temple, so the people must direct their prayers and attention there, also. Though God does not literally live in the Temple, it is the focal point of God's presence with the people. In later years Jews living in foreign lands turned toward Jerusalem to offer their prayers (see, for example, Daniel 6:10).

Verses 31-32: These verses may refer to legal cases in which there are no witnesses. The parties involved must appear in the Holy Place and swear that they are telling the truth. Anyone who swears falsely will bring disaster on himself (see Exodus 20:7).

Verse 40: The *fear* of God is intimately connected with love for God and with obedience to God (see, for example, Deuteronomy 6:2; 11:1). This fear is an awareness of the awesome qualities that belong to God alone and of the humble position of human beings in comparison. True love for and fear of God are the beginning of wisdom (see, for example, Psalm 111:10) and are the foundation for a righteous life.

Verse 51: Israel's slavery in Egypt is spoken of as an *iron furnace* (NIV; NRSV = *smelter*, see also Deuteronomy 4:20; Jeremiah 11:4) in which the people were severely tested and tried.

Benediction and Charge to the People (8:54-61)

Solomon tells the people that God has kept the promises made through their forefathers. They enjoy *rest* from God, which means that they have the land, its bounty, peace, and the means to enjoy all these benefits.

The people must fix their hearts on God and choose to live in obedience to their covenant responsibilities. In Old Testament thought, the heart is the place where all the forces of human life come together. These forces include emotion, intellect, will, and physical being. A person's character is shaped by the thoughts, plans, hopes, fears, and actions of the heart.

If the people of Israel are true to God, then God will

uphold them. Through the people of Israel, God will be revealed to the rest of the world.

Conclusion of the Dedication Feast (8:62-66)

The *sacrifice of fellowship* (NIV; NRSV = *sacrifice of well-being*) is part of the celebration feast and is a sign of well-being between God and the people. The people eat the cooked flesh of the sacrificial animals and the rest of the sacrifice is burned.

In the *burnt offering* the animal is burned whole. The *grain offering* is a vegetable or meal offering. All these sacrifices are so numerous that Solomon must consecrate the courtyard for burning the sacrifices as a substitute for the bronze altar.

§ § § § § § §

The Message of 1 Kings 5–8

The Temple in Jerusalem is the center of religious and national life in Israel from the construction of the First Temple by Solomon in 955 B.C. to the destruction of Herod's Temple in A.D. 70. Though the Babylonians destroyed Solomon's Temple in 587 B.C., the Jews who remained in Judah during the Babylonian exile continued to hold rituals and offer sacrifices in the Temple ruins. The Second Temple was completed in 515 B.C., and remodeled and expanded by King Herod (37–34 B.C.).

During these years, what role does the Temple play in the life of Israel?

§ Israel is a theocracy rather than a secular state. Thus, the Temple is the center of national as well as religious life in Israel.

§ The Temple is the "House of God" and, as such, is the site of God's special presence in and with Israel.

§ The Temple is the place toward which the prayers of the faithful are directed.

§ The Temple is the focal point of religious ritual and sacrifice. Daily sacrifices are offered, and there are special rituals and sacrifices on the sabbath and on each of the annual religious festivals.

Centuries after its destruction, the Temple remains a potent symbol of God's special presence in Jerusalem and with God's people. All that remains of either Temple is part of the southwestern retaining wall of Herod's temple. This is the western or "wailing" wall to which the faithful still come to pray in recognition of the tradition of prayer and worship that began on that site almost three thousand years ago.

§ § § § § § §

1 Kings 9–11

Introduction to These Chapters

These chapters tell of Solomon's reign, both his triumphs and his failures, after the Temple is built. The opening verses of chapter 9 set the standard by which the king is to be judged. The episodes that follow tell how well he lived up to this standard.

Here is an outline of these chapters.
  I. God Appears to Solomon (9:1-9)
  II. Building and Commercial Activities (9:10-28)
    A. Part of Galilee given to Hiram (9:10-14)
    B. Solomon's fortress- and store-cities (9:15-25)
    C. Solomon's trading fleet (9:26-28)
  III. Solomon and the Queen of Sheba (10:1-13)
  IV. Wealth and Business Activities (10:14-29)
  V. Solomon's Idolatry and Its Consequences (11:1-43)
    A. Foreign wives and idolatry (11:1-13)
    B. Solomon's adversaries (11:14-43)

God Appears to Solomon (9:1-9)

God responds to Solomon's prayers that were offered at the Temple dedication. The future will show that living faithfully under the covenant will bring the king and the people great rewards, but unfaithfulness will cost them dearly.

Verse 3: God has set aside the Temple as a holy place

that is blessed by the divine presence and has God's special attention.

Verses 4-9: The relationship between God and Israel requires faithfulness on both sides. Solomon must take the lead in righteous living as Israel's leader and God's servant on Israel's behalf. He must live under the law and abide by God's word. If he does not, both he and the people will suffer.

God warns Solomon against worshiping other gods. Idolatry is a violation of the first commandment (see Exodus 20:3) and undermines the heart of the covenant relationship. If the people of Israel are disloyal to God then all that David and Solomon worked for will be lost. Israel will lose the land and the Temple.

There is an understanding in Israel that God's promises concerning the permanence of the line of David and the Temple are not unconditional. In later generations, however, the people and the leaders take these promises for granted, with disastrous results (see, for example, Jeremiah 21:11–22:9).

Because of sin, Israel could become a proverbial object of scorn or of horror to other peoples instead of being a source of blessing (see, for example, Genesis 12:1-3; 1 Kings 8:59-60). In ancient times people would hiss to express contempt and also to ward off any evil spirits which might inhabit ruins.

If the people of Israel go after other gods, God will even allow the destruction of the Temple, the most visible sign of God's presence and power in Israel.

Part of Galilee Given to Hiram (9:10-14)

Solomon pays Hiram in agricultural goods for the timber used in his building projects (see 1 Kings 5:8-11). The large amount of gold he receives from Hiram may be used to finance his commercial ventures, since so much money goes into building the Temple and palace.

Hiram does not like the cities given to him. The district

of Cabul (which may mean *as nothing* or *displeasing*) may center around the town of Cabul in the hill country of lower Galilee. This area has plentiful oak forests, but it has few springs, poor soil, and is not well suited for agriculture.

A *talent* of gold weighs approximately seventy-five pounds and is worth approximately $30,000.

Solomon's Fortress- and Store-Cities (9:15-25)

Solomon's building projects are not confined to Jerusalem. He also constructs a series of fortress-cities and warehouse-cities by using slave labor.

Verses 15-19: The exact identity of the *Millo* (NRSV; NIV = *supporting terraces*) is not known. The word perhaps means *a filling* and indicates an earthwork south of the Temple that is part of the fortifications of Jerusalem.

Solomon expands existing towns and cities to suit his needs (see the Glossary for identification of these cities). The Israelite military has to hold onto the territory won by David and deal with rebellions within the empire. They must also guard the trade routes, which are the economic lifelines of the nation, from bandits and invaders.

The store-cities have warehouses for keeping provisions. These goods are probably for use by the military and for trade. The provincial capitals in each administrative district also have warehouses for collecting the taxable goods required to maintain Solomon's household and staff (see, for example, 1 Kings 4:26-28).

Verses 20-23: Some foreigners living in Israel are made permanent slaves of the state. (See the Glossary for identification of their countries.) Israelites are not permanent slaves but are required to give temporary labor to the state (see 1 Kings 5:13-16). This practice apparently continues even after the Temple and palace construction are finished. As part of the heavy burden placed on the Israelite people, this forced labor becomes a factor in the eventual rebellion of the northern tribes (see 1 Kings 12:1-18).

Verses 24-25: These verses are not directly related to the previous verses, but add details about the sequence of Solomon's construction projects (verse 24) and about his participation in Temple services (verse 25).

Three times a year refers to the major annual religious festivals. The Passover (or feast of Unleavened Bread) is held in the spring (March/April). The Harvest feast (or Pentecost) is held after the wheat harvest in June. The feast of Ingathering (or feast of Booths) is held after the fruit, grape, and olive harvest in the fall (September/October).

Solomon's Trading Fleet (9:26-28)

Solomon and Hiram cooperate in building and operating a merchant fleet. Its home port is on the Gulf of Aqaba on the northern end of the Red Sea. The exact location of Ophir is not known, but it is perhaps on the Red Sea coast of southern Arabia. In ancient times this area was famous for its gold and was on well-traveled trade routes (both overland and sea) between Arabia and India. Since a talent of gold is worth approximately $30,000, the fleet must take a tremendous amount of goods for trade. Copper may be one resource that the ships of Israel take to trade with other countries.

Solomon and the Queen of Sheba (10:1-13)

The Queen of Sheba has heard of Solomon's wisdom and wealth, and comes to judge for herself if all that she has heard is true. She probably also comes for business reasons. The land of Sheba is in southwestern Arabia, a region known for its wisdom and for its wealth of trade.

The queen asks Solomon *hard questions* or riddles. Such tests of intelligence, judgment, and wit are common in royal courts of the time. Solomon's powers and his grand household leave the queen *overwhelmed* (NIV; NRSV = *no more spirit in her*). She willingly acknowledges that he is an exceptional man.

The queen also undoubtedly speaks to Solomon about trade. Her country is a strong overland trading power, particularly in the spice and incense market. The northern end of the overland Arabian routes is in Israel and thus under Solomon's control. With Solomon's merchant fleet opening new sea trading routes to the south, the queen needs to strike some agreement with the king in order to protect her country's economic interests. Apparently she succeeds (verse 13).

Wealth and Business Activities (10:14-29)

Solomon is an accomplished businessman and a brilliant statesman. His skill brings in money and gifts both from trade and in tribute from other monarchs and governors (verses 15, 23-24). His ships go on three-year trading voyages bringing back goods from lands on both sides of the Red Sea. *Ships of Tarshish* (NRSV; NIV = *trading ships*) are large, oceangoing vessels made to withstand long, rough voyages.

Much of this treasure supports Solomon's lavish lifestyle. Much of it also must go into maintaining his large administration and military establishment (verse 26).

Solomon needs chariots and horses for his military, but neither is available in Israel. Egypt supplies the best chariots of the time and Kue (Cilicia in southeast Asia Minor) is the best source for horses. Since Israel controls the trade routes between the two sources, Solomon becomes a broker in this very lucrative trade.

Foreign Wives and Idolatry (11:1-13)

The fact that Solomon loves many women and has an extraordinary number of wives is in keeping with his stature as king and with his time. The problem with these wives lies in the fact that some of them are from nations with whom Israelites are forbidden to marry (see Deuteronomy 7:1-5), and in the fact that they influence Solomon to worship pagan gods. The writers of Kings see this idolatry as the source of trouble within Solomon's reign and as the cause of the division of the kingdom at his death. None of the material in this chapter appears in Second Chronicles. The Chronicler's history of Israel casts a more favorable light on Solomon's reign.

Verses 1-8: Many of these marriages are for political purposes to establish alliances between Solomon and neighboring monarchs (see, for example, 1 Kings 3:1). Out of his attachment to these wives, Solomon begins to worship their gods.

Ashtoreth (or *Astarte*) is a Phoenician goddess of love and fertility. *Milcom* (or *Molech*) is the national god of the Ammonites. *Chemosh* is the god of Moab.

Verses 9-13: God will allow a king in the line of David to stay on the throne in Jerusalem, but Solomon has forfeited most of his kingdom because of his disobedience. The *one tribe* is the tribe of Judah which will maintain control of the territory of Judah, including Jerusalem.

The reasons given here for the breakup of the kingdom of Israel are related to the warnings against the monarchy given by Samuel (see 1 Samuel 8:1-18) and by the Deuteronomic historians (see Deuteronomy 17:14-20). Problems within the reign of Solomon are especially evident in the warnings issued in the Deuteronomy passage.

Solomon's Adversaries (11:14-43)

According to the writers of Kings, Solomon's troubles with political and military rivals come from his unfaithfulness to God.

Verses 14-22: Hadad survives David's takeover of

Edom as a refugee in Egypt. He returns home and causes much *trouble* for Solomon (see verse 25), perhaps controlling some of the more remote regions of the country. He apparently does not take over complete control of Edom, however, because Solomon maintains his merchant fleet base at Ezion-geber in Edom (1 Kings 9:26).

Verses 23-25: Solomon loses some of the Syrian territory won by David (see 2 Samuel 8:3-6; 10:15-19). He may, however, maintain some control over the land and the important caravan routes that run from northern Israel northeastward toward the Euphrates River.

Verses 26-40: Jeroboam comes to Solomon's attention as an able and hard-working young man, so he is put in charge of the labor gangs conscripted from the ten tribes living in northern Israel (*the house of Joseph*). The prophet Ahijah, from Shiloh in northern Israel, brings Jeroboam an oracle from God (*thus says the* LORD) which designates him as the new king of the northern tribes. The *one tribe* saved for the house of David is Judah (this probably also includes parts of the tribes of Benjamin and Simeon that are associated with Judah). The house of David will *always have a lamp* (that is, will be a light or life) to serve God in Jerusalem.

Jeroboam accepts his prophetic appointment (Saul and David were also named king by a prophet). He may make his first moves of rebellion against Solomon during the time Solomon is repairing the wall of Jerusalem (verse 27). Solomon is strong enough to stop the plot for the time being, but not forever.

Verses 41-43: The book of the Acts of Solomon is an account of Solomon's reign and achievements from which the writers of Kings draw material for their history.

§ § § § § § §

The Message of 1 Kings 9–11

Any evaluation of Solomon's reign must include the changes, both positive and negative, that come about in Israel during this time.

§ Most of the territory gained by David is held and consolidated into the Israelite state.

§ Many civil, military, and religious construction projects, including the Temple in Jerusalem, are completed in all areas of the country.

§ Trade and commerce increase dramatically.

§ Wisdom, music, and literature flourish.

§ Many people enjoy a newfound prosperity.

§ Class differences also widen. Many poor people do not share in the new prosperity.

§ The people endure forced labor and heavy taxes.

§ The state rather than the covenant is now the focal point of national obligation.

§ Solomon officially introduces foreign cults into Israel.

The problems of idolatry and social injustice are evident in Solomon's reign, and these problems continue to plague both Israel and Judah.

At the heart of the matter seems to be the desire of the people of Israel to "be like all the nations." Time and again the king and the people give in to the pull of worshiping their neighbors' gods and to accumulating power and riches like their neighbors. They struggle to maintain their calling as God's chosen people. It is one thing to make a covenant with God when you are a poor, powerless band of ex-slaves. Living out this covenant relationship when you are more in control of your life is more difficult.

§ § § § § § §

1 Kings 12–14

Introduction to These Chapters

Long-held differences of opinion, old rivalries, and tensions between the tribes come to a head after Solomon's death. One last chance for the United Kingdom to survive is wasted by Solomon's son, Rehoboam. Israel becomes two nations that are sometimes at war with one another and sometimes at peace, though both are weaker in comparison to the United Kingdom. The new nation of Israel survives until 722 B.C. when it is absorbed into the Assyrian empire. The nation of Judah survives until 597 B.C. when it is taken over by Babylonia.

These chapters may be outlined as follows.
  I. Greater Israel Is Divided (12:1-33)
     A. Rehoboam will not relent (12:1-24)
     B. Jeroboam sets up his kingdom (12:25-33)
 II. A Judean Prophet Condemns Jeroboam (13:1-34)
III. The End of Jeroboam's Reign (14:1-20)
 IV. The Reign of Rehoboam (14:21-30)

Rehoboam Will Not Relent (12:1-24)

After his father's death, Rehoboam is acclaimed king in Judah, and then travels to Shechem in northern Israel to be officially accepted by the northern tribes. The northern Israelites and even Jeroboam are ready to accept Rehoboam as king and are willing to keep the country together, if Rehoboam will discontinue some of the burdensome obligations that Solomon imposed on the people.

The *heavy yoke* refers to the burden of taxes that Solomon required for the maintenance of his household and of his administration (see 1 Kings 4:7-28). The *yoke* also includes the forced labor that Israelites are required to give to the state (see 1 Kings 5:13-16).

Rehoboam's older and wiser counselors advise him to remember that, as king, he is the *servant* of the people as well as the head of state (see also 1 Kings 8:24, 28). The king has the special responsibility of serving Israel on God's behalf. He must serve God and must lead and protect his people. The people in turn are the king's servants in the sense that they support him and follow his lead. All the people of Israel, including kings, priests, prophets, and people, are God's servants. Servant and master have a personal relationship in which the servant has an humble appreciation for his or her role and place within the established order.

The terms of the relationship between God and Israel are given in the covenant. No one in Israel, not even the king, is exempt from the covenant law. It would seem that Rehoboam does not understand or acknowledge this larger perspective in which he is granted the right to rule over Israel.

Rehoboam listens to his younger advisors and offers no compromise to the northern tribes. He arrogantly declares himself to be stronger and more virile than Solomon and promises to best his father at imposing burdens on the people. *Scorpions* are a particularly cruel type of lash.

The writers of Kings credit Rehoboam's disastrous decision to the influence of God (verse 15; also 11:31-39).

The northern Israelites' reply to Rehoboam (verse 16) is similar to revolutionary words spoken against David (see 2 Samuel 20:1). This is an indication of the divisions among the tribes of Israel that neither David nor Solomon could eliminate.

Rehoboam compounds his errors by sending Adoram, head of the labor gangs, presumably to help settle the situation. This costs Adoram his life and forces Rehoboam to flee back to Jerusalem. A civil war is prevented only by a word from God through the prophet Shemaiah.

Jeroboam Sets Up His Kingdom (12:25-33)

Jeroboam moves to strengthen his position both militarily and politically. He fortifies Shechem and makes it his capital. Penuel, to the east of the Jordan River, is fortified as a defense against invaders from the east.

Jeroboam uses religion and worship as means to reinforce his people's loyalties to the new northern kingdom. He constructs shrines for worship and sacrifice in the north so the people will not go to the Temple in Jerusalem. The two golden calves recall the people to their ancestral days of wandering in the wilderness (see Exodus 32:4-8). The calves may not be looked upon as idols or gods in and of themselves, but as thrones or pedestals for the invisible God (as is the ark of the covenant in the Temple).

Regardless of their exact function, these images are condemned by the Deuteronomic historians (verse 30), are outlawed by the covenant (see Deuteronomy 5:8-9), and are associated with certain Canaanite fertility cults.

Houses on high places are cultic shrines.

The writers also condemn Jeroboam for celebrating the fall harvest festival in the eighth month instead of the seventh (see Leviticus 23:34), and for celebrating at the calf shrine.

A Judean Prophet Condemns Jeroboam (13:1-34)

The story in this chapter falls into two main parts: (1) a prophet from Judah comes to Bethel and announces God's judgment against the altar which Jeroboam built;

and (2) the prophet is disobedient to God's word and dies near Bethel.

There are indications that the writers of Kings may have added details to this older story that update the story from their later perspective. The reference to *Josiah* (verse 2) may have been added after the religious reforms that he carried out during his reign (640-609 B.C.). Verse 2 would still make sense without the king's name. It would then just tell of a future king from Judah who would be more faithful to God than Jeroboam is. The other later addition may be the reference to *Samaria* (verse 32). The city of Samaria, which became the capital of the Northern Kingdom, was not built until approximately 870 B.C. by King Omri (see 1 Kings 16:24), and the surrounding territory was not called Samaria until after the city was built.

The overall theme of the story is that God will deal with disobedience. The immediate context of the story is the sinful situation in the Northern Kingdom under Jeroboam's leadership. The writers of Kings report the story as evidence that Jeroboam is warned about his sinful ways and is even healed by God's mercy but still does not *turn from his evil way.*

Verses 1-10: The *man of God* is a prophet and delivers a true message in contrast to the *old prophet* of Bethel (verse 11), who appears to be a false prophet.

Destruction of the altar will put an end to the improper worship taking place at the shrine. Burning human bones on the altar will make it unclean and unfit for cultic use. The altar breaks apart as a sign of the complete destruction that will come in later years.

Jeroboam offers the man of God his hospitality and a gift after the king's hand is healed. The man refuses Jeroboam's offer because to eat and drink with someone and to accept that person's hospitality is a symbol of friendship and loyalty. The man of God from Judah must not in any way seem to approve of what the king is doing.

Verses 11-32: The story does not say why the Bethel prophet lies to the Judean prophet. Perhaps he does it as a test of whether the Judean prophet is false or true.

The confirmation that the Judean is truly a *man of God* comes when he is killed on his way home. Because he disobeyed God, he will not have the comfort and honor of dying at home and being buried with his ancestors (verses 21-22).

The prophet of Bethel asks to be buried with his brother prophet because he now knows that the man spoke the true word of God. This shows the bond that exists between those who recognize the true word of God, whether they are from Israel or from Judah.

Verses 33-34: Jeroboam perhaps thinks that the message of the Judean prophet is not true since the man dies before leaving Israel. Whatever his reasons, the king continues in his sin. The altar at Bethel is rebuilt, but it is destroyed by Josiah (see 2 Kings 23:15-18). Because of Jeroboam's guilt, his family ends with the death of his son Nadab (see 1 Kings 15:25-30).

The End of Jeroboam's Reign (14:1-20)

Jeroboam sends his wife to consult with the prophet Ahijah, who had previously decreed that Jeroboam was to be king of Israel (see 1 Kings 11:29-39). Ahijah has an oracle from God that is an announcement of judgment on Jeroboam. Because of Jeroboam's sins, his son, Abijah, will die and his other male heirs will be wiped out.

An oracle is a message or announcement from God. Such announcements can either be of judgment or of hope. In their classic form, prophetic announcements of judgment have three basic parts:
1. an introduction or call to attention,
2. a description of sins, and
3. a proclamation of punishment.
Not all oracles of judgment have all three parts. Some

have all the parts but in a different order (see, for example, Jeremiah 2:4-13; Amos 1:3-5; 3:1-2).

Judgment is announced because of specific failures on the part of the people of Israel in general, or on the part of a particular individual, such as Jeroboam. The listing of these failures shows that God's judgment is rational and just. The announcement of judgment begins the process by which judgment is carried out (see also discussion of prophetic speech in the comments on 1 Kings 18:17-19).

Prophetic oracles often begin with the phrases *Hear the word of the Lord* or *Thus says the Lord*. They often end with *declares the Lord* or *the Lord has spoken it*. These phrases alert the listeners, and the readers, to the authority of the prophets' words.

In Ahijah's words to Jeroboam, the parts of the oracle are as follows:

1. call to attention, verse 7*a*;
2. description of sins, reasons for judgment, verses 7-9;
3. proclamation of punishment, verses 10-11.

God is angry with Jeroboam because the king turned his back on God (*thrust me behind your back*). This has the sense of a deliberate turning away, putting God "out of sight and out of mind."

The death of Abijah is an example of the principle that the sins of fathers will be visited on their children (see Exodus 20:5; Numbers 14:18; also 2 Samuel 12:13-15). In later years, this principle is modified so that persons are held accountable only for their own righteousness or sin (see Ezekiel 18:1-20).

Jewish rabbis teach that Abijah finds favor with God because he does not support Jeroboam's efforts to keep the people from worshiping in Jerusalem.

Jeroboam's sins will affect not only his family but all Israel as well (verses 14-16). *Beyond the River* (NIV; NRSV = *Euphrates*) refers to the deportation of many Israelites after Assyria took over Israel in 722 B.C. Jeroboam sets an example for idol worship (*Asherim*) which most Israelite kings unfortunately follow until the destruction of the kingdom by Assyria in 722 B.C.

The Reign of Rehoboam (14:21-30)

The people of Judah, under Rehoboam's leadership, are also unfaithful to God like the Israelites (see also 2 Chronicles 12).

Verses 21-24: They are involved in idol worship and fertility cult practices, which they copy from the pagans who still live in Judah.

Cult prostitutes (both male and female) are part of fertility cult rituals in which sexual intercourse is believed to have a magical power to ensure the fertility of the land and the people. Later prophets, such as Hosea, Jeremiah, and Ezekiel, speak out against the continuing practice of idol worship in Israel and Judah.

God is *jealous* because the people of Judah are unfaithful to their covenant vows (see Exodus 20:2-5). God's holiness, zeal, and love for the chosen people turn to jealousy and anger when they stray from their proper relationship to God.

Verses 25-31: Egypt's campaign against Judah (also against parts of Israel) is confirmed in Egyptian historical records. Temple and palace treasures are given in tribute to the Egyptians. Rehoboam cannot maintain all the riches of Solomon's kingdom.

The *war* between Rehoboam and Jeroboam (verse 30) is probably limited to border disputes and skirmishes rather than being a full-scale war.

§ § § § § § §

The Message of 1 Kings 12–14

Jeroboam is designated by God through the prophet Ahijah to be king of Israel. The new king betrays this trust, however, by promoting idol worship, and he falls far short of the standards set for the kings of Israel (see "The Message of 1 Kings 1–2"). Instead, Jeroboam sets a standard for disobedience to which future Israelite kings are compared (see, for example, 2 Kings 15:8-9). Jeroboam's sin provokes God to anger or wrath. What does the Old Testament say about the wrath of God?

§ The understanding of God's wrath is determined by faith in a divine, personal God rather than in an impersonal, irrational force.

§ God's wrath is a process or emotion in God as it is in human beings. God's wrath is distinguished from human anger by its power and scope.

§ The objects of God's wrath are individuals and nations (both Israel and others).

§ God's wrath is aroused by sin (such as idolatry, injustice, arrogance, and wickedness), which opposes God's holy will.

§ God's wrath is exercised in relation to and in balance with divine justice, zeal, and love.

§ The aim of God's wrath is the establishment of holiness. It is not just punishment, but is to set things right in the world.

§ § § § § § §

1 Kings 15–16

Introduction to These Chapters

These chapters tell about the reigns of the kings of
Israel and Judah from Jeroboam and Abijam to Omri and
Asa (1 Kings 15:1–16:28), and they begin the report of the
reign of King Ahab of Israel (1 Kings 16:29-34).

They may be outlined as follows.

The Reign of Abijam (15:1-8)

This king is referred to in some manuscripts as *Abijah*.
The writers of Kings do not report much about his reign
except that he followed in the same sins as his father,
Rehoboam (see 1 Kings 14:21-24). Rehoboam's mother
was an Ammonite princess, and Abijam's mother (the
granddaughter of Absalom, here called *Abishalom*) is a
worshiper of Asherah (see verse 12). Foreign influences
within the royal household foster tolerance and support
for pagan religious practices, both in the royal family and
in Judah at large.

The Reign of Asa (15:9-24)

Asa has a long reign and receives a favorable evaluation from the historians of Kings (see also 2 Chronicles 14:1–16:14). It is not clear whether Asa is Abijam's son (as in verse 8) or his brother (as in verses 2, 10). Asa may be Abijam's son who comes to the throne as a boy when Abijam dies prematurely. If Asa's mother is also dead, then Maacah would remain as queen mother.

Asa goes a long way in eliminating idol worship from Judah, even though he does not destroy all the shrines on high places. As further evidence that Asa is a true follower of the Lord, he brings royal gifts to the Temple. These votive gifts are set aside for sacred use. They are given along with a vow or promise from the giver in the expectation that God will bless the giver.

Verses 16-22: Baasha comes practically to Asa's doorstep at Ramah, which is only five miles north of Jerusalem near the border between Israel and Judah. This fortress controls the main road from north to south and the main road toward the coastal plain.

Asa bribes the king of Syria to attack Israel and relieve the pressure which Israel is putting on Judah. This strategy is successful both for Syria and Judah. Asa uses the materials captured at Ramah and forced labor from among his subjects to build other fortresses farther north.

Asa comes under criticism in 2 Chronicles 16:7-14, particularly for his failure to seek God's help with his foot disease.

The Reign of Nadab (15:25-28)

The writers of Kings now turn their attention to the kings of Israel: Nadab, Baasha, Elah, Zimri, and Omri (1 Kings 15:25–16:28) and Ahab (1 Kings 16:29–22:40).

The custom of a king's son following him on the throne is not as firmly established in Israel as in Judah. Israel is a nation made up of ten tribes, whereas Judah is basically one tribe which has an undisputed center of power in Jerusalem and an undisputed family line on the throne. Nadab, Elah, and Zimri all die violently in the continuing struggle for the throne of Israel.

Baasha may be one of Nadab's army officers who uses the Israelite attack on a Philistine city as an opportunity to kill the king. He then ruthlessly kills all of Jeroboam's family, apparently exceeding the prophecy which says that only the male descendants will die (see 1 Kings 14:10). The historian of Kings sees this as the result of Jeroboam's sins (verse 30).

The Reign of Baasha (15:29–16:7)

Baasha has been made a *leader* of Israel by divine decree, as was Jeroboam (see 1 Kings 11:30-37). Also like Jeroboam, Baasha is condemned in a prophetic announcement of judgment (verses 2-4).

Verses 2, 7: The reasons for God's judgment on Baasha are given in these two verses. Baasha follows the example of Jeroboam by promoting idol worship and unfaithfulness to God. Baasha also goes beyond the proclaimed punishment of Jeroboam's house (see 1 Kings 14:10). Instead of killing only the males in Jeroboam's family, Baasha destroys all the house of Jeroboam.

The Reign of Elah (16:8-14)

Elah reigns only a few months from (approximately) the end of 877 B.C. into the first months of 876 B.C. He is thus given credit for reigning two years. Zimri, an army commander, takes advantage of Elah's drunken state to strike him down. After killing the rest of Baasha's male family members and friends, Zimri may suppose that he has eliminated the competition for the throne and that he has enough support in the military to stay in power.

The writers of Kings see this as fulfillment of the prophecy spoken against the house of Baasha (verses 12-13; see also verses 2-4).

The Reign of Zimri (16:15-20)

Zimri reigns only seven days before he is overthrown by another part of the Israelite military. Omri is a general of the army, and the troops in the field with him (not yet literally all Israel) proclaim him king when they hear that Zimri has murdered Elah. When Zimri realizes that his cause is lost, he commits suicide.

Zimri does not reign long enough to exert much leadership in Israel either for good or evil. The writers of Kings, however, include their standard denunciation of northern kings (verse 19) in their evaluation of his reign.

The Reign of Omri (16:21-28)

Four or five years of civil war follow Zimri's death. Omri finally secures the throne and is proclaimed king over Israel.

The relatively short report of Omri's reign does not include many of his accomplishments as king. The writers of Kings are more interested in a religious evaluation of his reign than in the political side.

Omri is an able and vigorous leader who is recognized as such by other nations and who makes peace with Judah. Long after his death, Assyrian records still refer to Israel as "the land of the house of Omri." Omri brings Moab under Israelite control and receives tribute from them. There is no direct biblical reference to this conquest, but there is a record of the amount of tribute paid and of Moab's successful revolt against Israel in later years (see 2 Kings 3:4). Historical records from Moab tell how Moab is afflicted by Israel for many years.

Omri makes an alliance with Phoenicia, as did David and Solomon. This alliance is sealed by the marriage of Omri's son, Ahab, to the Phoenician princess, Jezebel. The alliance works to Israel's advantage economically by increasing trade, but it will have disastrous long-term results both religiously and politically because of Jezebel's influence on the nation.

Omri also moves his capital from Tirzah to Samaria, which is in the central hills of Palestine approximately forty-two miles north of Jerusalem. The city occupies an easily defensible site above fertile valleys and hills. It also overlooks the main road from Jerusalem into northern Israel. Construction on Samaria continues on into the reign of Ahab. Only the fortification foundation stones of this royal citadel remain, but they give evidence that the city was beautifully designed and well constructed. Ivory inlays found among the ruins also show the richness of royal and governmental life there.

The writers of Kings give no reasons for their negative judgment of Omri except the usual report that he is like Jeroboam (verses 25-26). Their greatest case against him probably comes from the marriage of Ahab and Jezebel, which fosters the already-established tolerance for foreign cults in Israel.

Ahab Becomes King (16:29-34)

Ahab's reign is dealt with in much greater detail than those of other Israelite kings. This first section in the text tells of the Canaanite god and goddess he worships. These cults will lead to a confrontation between Ahab and Jezebel on one side and the prophets Elijah and Elisha on the other.

In Hebrew *baal* means *the lord, the owner*, and can refer to various pagan gods. In this case, baal probably refers to Melqart, the god of Tyre who is believed to be the lord of the underworld.

Hiel is probably given authority by Ahab to rebuild Jericho. Israelite forces under Joshua had destroyed Jericho's fortifications (see Joshua 6), but the town remained settled to some extent. According to the historians of Kings, Hiel loses his sons to the curse that Joshua put on Jericho (see Joshua 6:26).

§ § § § § § §

The Message of 1 Kings 15–16

Omri and his descendants bring Israel a measure of internal stability, strength in relation to her neighbors, and economic prosperity. There is a darker side of his reign, however, that the writers of Kings touch on only indirectly when they refer to Omri's idolatry (verses 25-26). Israel becomes stronger in some ways, but she is weaker in her relationship with God and in the quality of life for many of her inhabitants.

Economic and religious abuses plague both Israel and Judah until the end of their lives as nations. Indeed, later prophets such as Amos and Jeremiah link the failure of economic and social justice to the failure of the people and their leaders to live up to the responsibilities of their faith.

What is the relationship between justice and righteousness (or, between daily life and faith)?

§ In the Old Testament, justice and righteousness are inseparable.

§ Righteousness is being in right relationship to God.

§ Justice is the maintenance of this right relationship.

§ This right relationship is founded on the covenant made between God and the chosen people.

§ Covenant law defines the way this relationship is to be put into practice in daily life. This includes the relationship between people and God as well as the relationships people have with one another.

§ No one, neither king nor commoner, is outside of the obligations of the law.

§ The covenant and the law would not exist without God's mercy and grace. Therefore, mercy and grace are necessary parts of justice and righteousness.

§ § § § § § §

1 Kings 17–19

Introduction to These Chapters

Much of the material about the reign of Ahab focuses on the prophet Elijah and on the religious situation in Israel during this time. Chapters 17–19 tell stories about Elijah's prophetic activities and about his relationship with Ahab and Jezebel. The end of chapter 19 tells about Elisha's call to prophesy.

Here is an outline of these chapters.
    I. Elijah, Ahab, and Jezebel (17:1–19:3)
        A. Elijah and the famine from God (17:1-24)
        B. Elijah and the prophets of Baal (18:1–19:3)
   II. Elijah and Elisha (19:4-21)

Elijah and the Famine From God (17:1-24)

The story in this chapter introduces Elijah and shows that he is truly "a man of God." This sets the stage for the other stories about him and also establishes his authority as a prophet, one who has been called by God. Even his name, which means "Yah(weh) is God," is symbolic of his calling.

Elijah is called to speak God's word and act on God's behalf in a new and trying situation in the life of Israel. Ahab's ascension to the throne gives Jezebel, the queen, new power and incentive to establish her religion as the dominant and official faith in Israel. She is loyal to her faith and aggressive in her efforts to promote it. She has no interest in or loyalty to the covenant faith of Israel. Ahab, on the other hand, apparently does not completely abandon his faith in God but seeks to worship God and his wife's gods at the same time. The result is that, for the first time in Israel's history, those who speak out in God's name against the policies of the king are subject to persecution.

Verses 1-7: God sends Elijah to Ahab with a message concerning a drought that will afflict Israel and other surrounding areas. The exact extent of the drought is not known, but it must have caused great hardship and suffering. Throughout the history of Israel and of Judah, many people lived barely above subsistence level so that the threat of starvation because of drought and famine was always great. Luke 4:24-26 states that the drought lasted three and one-half years. The Jewish historian Josephus refers to a drought during this time which lasted a year.

The motive behind the drought is to prove that God, and not the pagan gods, is in control of the rain. The Phoenician god Baal-Melqart is believed by his worshipers to be the one who controls the rain. The drought and the subsequent rain (see 1 Kings 18:1) will show that God is the one in control, not only of the weather, but also of Israel's destiny.

God sends Elijah out of Ahab's territory for protection from the king and sends him food. Though the personal cost of prophecy is often high for Elijah (see, for example, 1 Kings 19:1-4) and for other prophets (see, for example, Jeremiah 20:14-18), God provides for the needs of those who are called to God's service.

Verses 8-16: God now sends Elijah into Phoenician territory, where he will be safe from Ahab. This area is also affected by drought. The widow's willingness to aid Elijah is rewarded by God. As a result of her actions, she and her household are given enough food to see them through the crisis.

Verses 17-24: When the widow's son becomes ill and dies, she believes that Elijah's presence in her home has brought God so close to her that God has found some secret sin in her. She thinks this sin has caused her child's death. There is a widely held view in ancient times that sickness and death are punishment for sin. Elijah's anguished question to God in verse 20 reflects this same view.

Elijah prays to God to restore the child's life, and he stretches himself out on the child (compare Elisha's actions in 2 Kings 4:34-37), making his body a vessel through which the power of God restores life to the child's body.

The widow's confession in verse 24 confirms Elijah's authority as a prophet.

Elijah and the Prophets of Baal (18:1–19:3)

God decides to end the drought and so sends Elijah to Ahab with the message to expect rain.

Verses 1-16: All the time Elijah has been out of Israel Ahab has been searching for him. Obadiah, an official in the king's household, has been trying to serve God and serve the king. He has helped save prophets who are loyal to God from Jezebel's wrath. These are probably groups of prophets who are associated with shrines to God in Israel (see 2 Kings 2:2-5) or who travel around the countryside prophesying (see 1 Samuel 10:5-13). Given the dangerous situation in which those loyal to God find themselves, it is not surprising that Obadiah requires Elijah to give him special reassurance that he will not be killed by the king.

Verses 17-19: Ahab accuses Elijah of stirring up trouble in Israel. Behind this accusation are Ahab's beliefs that he can practice both worship of God and worship of idols without being subject to God's wrath. Ahab also believes in the power of Elijah's words to make things happen, else the king would not try so hard to get Elijah to keep quiet.

In the Old Testament, prophetic speech is believed to have creative power. Behind this power is the creative power of God's word (see, for example, the power of the word in Genesis 1). According to Old Testament tradition, this power extends to God's word spoken by a prophet. The prophetic word is not spoken to speculate about or to predict the future, but is spoken to make known God's will for the present or the future. The prophet tells his listeners of God's intentions, and his words set in motion the process of carrying out those intentions. The prophetic word acts to make things happen.

The Israelites believed that oracles (prophetic messages) and demonstrations of God's words possessed a power that set in motion the accomplishment of God's word. Language was seen as a dynamic force that could affect the physical world. Thus, the fulfillment of the prophetic word begins with the spoken word of the prophet. Given the power granted to the true prophetic word, those who oppose the word spoken by a prophet would naturally want the prophet to be silent or might accuse the prophet of deliberately bringing trouble on those against whom he speaks.

Verses 20-40: Ahab agrees to a test of power between the pagan gods and the Lord God of Israel. It is not only the king but also the people of Israel who are dividing their loyalties between God and idols. Elijah's question to them in verse 21 reflects the fact that they weaken themselves by trying to follow both types of faith. To *go limping with two different opinions* (NRSV) is in Hebrew to *go hopping on the two boughs*. This has the sense of hopping from one leg to another or waivering *between two opinions* (NIV). Elijah confronts the people of Israel with the fact that they must decide who is really God and then believe and act accordingly.

Verses 22-38: The test will be to see which god will bring rain, and the sign will be, not water, but fire. The one who sends the fire and then the rain is the one who controls the fertility of the land and the destiny of its people.

The pagan prophets go through a frenzied ritual of leaping, dancing, shouting, and cutting themselves, but their ravings do no good. They get only Elijah's mockery in return.

The *altar of the* LORD may have been torn down by pagan worshipers. The repaired altar rests on stones that are symbolic of all the tribes of Israel, who are called and named (and thus claimed) by God. The water that is poured on the offering may be to ritually clean the altar. It may also be a symbol of the rain that is to come as a result of the sacrifice.

In Verse 36, the *oblation* (NRSV) is a gift, or *sacrifice* (NIV), and the *time* is about 3:00 P.M.

Elijah has the pagan prophets killed because he is in a Holy War against paganism. Just as when the Israelites first entered Canaan, they still face a threat from the temptations offered by pagan cults (see Deuteronomy 20:16-18). If the people give in to the worship of other gods, it will mean the end of their existence as God's people. Thus, harsh measures are often taken in this life and death struggle for the hearts and minds of the people of Israel.

Verses 41-46: Elijah waits for a sign of the coming rains and then warns Ahab to get home ahead of the downpour. Jezreel is located on the plain of Esdraelon, which can become impassable during heavy rains. Elijah runs ahead of Ahab approximately seventeen miles to Jezreel. The *hand of the* LORD, that is, the power of God, is with Elijah to give him both spiritual and physical strength.

Verses 19:1-3: Elijah flees from Jezebel's reach. The hand of God is still with him, however, because he is given sufficient warning to escape and because God finds him and gives him new commissions to carry out (see 1 Kings 19:4-18).

Elijah and Elisha (19:4-21)

Verses 4-8: Elijah goes to the Judean wilderness and waits to die. He apparently feels that he has failed in his prophetic duties despite his success at Mount Carmel. He must realize from Jezebel's threat toward him that the battle for the hearts of the king and the people of Israel is not yet won. God sends an angel to minister to Elijah's physical hunger so that he has the strength to travel on.

Verses 9-14: Elijah travels to Mount Horeb (another name for Mount Sinai). This is where Moses received the Ten Commandments and where the people of Israel entered into a covenant relationship with God.

Elijah confesses to God that he has been loyal and zealous in his duties on God's behalf. Now, however, he feels alone and helpless against the forces that oppose his message.

Earthquake, wind, and fire are natural forces associated with God's appearance on earth (see also, for example, Ezekiel 1:4, 26-28; Micah 1:3-4). God is not found in any of these natural forces, however; they only precede God's coming. God is found in the message to the prophet, and, further, in the prophetic message to God's people.

Verses 15-18: Elijah is to authorize Hazael, Jehu, and Elisha to carry out the duties assigned to them by God. Elisha eventually succeeds Elijah and is the one who fulfills the assignment God gives Elijah concerning Hazael (see 2 Kings 8:7-15) and Jehu (see 2 Kings 9:1-3).

God tells Elijah that a righteous *remnant* of the faithful will be left alive in Israel. In the Old Testament the number seven is often used in settings where it symbolizes perfection and consummation. The number 7,000, as a multiple of seven, here symbolizes those in

Israel who have remained true to their faith and with whom lies the hope for Israel's future.

Verses 19-21: Elisha is in a field plowing with other workers. They are each plowing with a pair of oxen, and they work in a row across the field.

Elisha (whose name means *God is salvation*) realizes the significance of receiving Elijah's mantle. This is his anointing into prophetic service, and with it he accepts Elijah's commission. The mantle is a cape or loose coat that is probably made of goat's skin with the hair turned outward.

Elijah gives Elisha permission to tell his parents goodbye. The last sentence in verse 20 has been interpreted to mean "Go, and return to me, for I have done something very important to you," or perhaps "Go back. I am not stopping you."

Elisha's sacrifice of the oxen is a thank-offering for his call to prophesy which he shares with his neighbors. He becomes both Elijah's helper and apprentice who is now authorized to carry on as God's messenger after Elijah is taken away.

§ § § § § § §

The Message of 1 Kings 17–19

These chapters show us two different parts of Elijah's life as a prophet. There are times when, as God's representative to the people of Israel, he brings life out of death (chapter 17) and he demonstrates God's power over creation (chapter 18). There are also times, however, when Elijah feels afraid and weak and is overwhelmed by the forces working against him (chapter 19). Such contrasts are typical of the lives of many Old Testament prophets. They are called and compelled to speak God's word and to demonstrate God's power, but they do not always feel successful in their work. What do these stories about Elijah tell us about the life and ministry of a prophet?

§ Prophets speak at God's direction within specific historical situations.

§ Prophetic messages are not just theoretical, but are related to life and death issues in the lives of God's people.

§ The purpose of prophetic speech and actions is to make known God's will and to begin the process of carrying out God's will.

§ The prophetic call is not to be taken lightly. The prophet can face personal opposition and threat as well as opposition to the prophetic word.

§ God calls to prophesy even those people who feel unprepared or who feel that they have failed in their assigned task.

§ God prepares the prophet for his or her task and watches over the prophet's life.

§ § § § § § §

1 Kings 20–22

Introduction to These Chapters

These last chapters in First Kings tell about the last years of Ahab's reign and the beginning of the reign of his son, Ahaziah. They may be outlined as follows.

I. Ahab's Wars With Syria (20:1-43)
II. Naboth's Vineyard (21:1-29)
III. Ahab, Jehoshaphat, and Ahaziah (22:1-53)
    A. Ahab's war against Syria (22:1-40)
    B. Jehoshaphat and Ahaziah (22:41-53)

Ahab's Wars With Syria (20:1-43)

The exact dates of these conflicts between Israel and Syria are not known. These events probably happened not long before 853 B.C. when the Israelites and the Syrians fought together against the invading Assyrians.

Chapter 20 opens in the midst of hostilities between Ahab and Benhadad, the king of Syria. The Arameans of Syria had long been a rival power to Israel. Syrian forces have apparently been successful in gaining a foothold in Israel, because Ahab addresses Benhadad as his overlord. The Syrians had previously taken some Israelite territory and gained trade advantages in Samaria, perhaps early in the reign of Omri. Now Benhadad is pressing to completely overwhelm Israel. Ahab successfully meets the threat, however, and Israel is victorious over Syria, at least for the time being.

The writers of Kings may have drawn on two different

historical sources for the material in chapter 20. Verses 1-34 seem to be from a source that is favorable to Ahab and that approves of his conduct of the war against Syria. Verses 35-43, however, are critical of Ahab's leniency toward the Syrian king.

Verses 1-12: Benhadad receives a verbal acknowledgement from Ahab that Ahab is his vassal (verses 3-4). He also probably receives tribute (gold, silver, or other treasures) from Ahab. Benhadad is not satisfied with this and presses for Ahab to literally give up his family and treasures (verses 5-6). Ahab is not willing to let Benhadad have this much power over him or humiliate him to this extent. The elders and other people in Israel back Ahab's refusal, and the country prepares for war.

Ahab and Benhadad then trade threats and insults (verses 10-11). Benhadad wishes defeat and humiliation on himself if he does not reduce Samaria to such ruins that the city will not provide even a handful of dust for each of his soldiers. Ahab replies that the time for boasting is not before the battle but after the battle is won.

Verses 13-21: Ahab first attacks with a small commando-type group of 232 warriors, and then follows up with other troops to rout the Syrians. Though greatly outnumbered, the Israelites will win. They will win because of God's strength and God's will, not because of their own strength or virtue. The purpose of this defeat is to increase their knowledge of and faithfulness to God (*you shall know that I am the* LORD).

The *young men* of the provincial governors are young men from each of the administrative districts in Israel.

Verses 22-30: The Syrians come back to attack Israel again in the spring. The Syrians do not understand that the God of Israel is universal and is not a local god. They think that they can win over Israel if they fight the battle out of the home territory of Israel's "gods."

This particular city named Aphek may be on the coastal Plain of Sharon fifteen miles northwest of Samaria.

Again, Israel's victory will increase their knowledge of God. This will be a sign to them and to the Syrians that the God of Israel is victorious no matter where the battle is fought or how many warriors are on God's side.

The wall *collapsing* (verse 30) may indicate that the city wall was destroyed and, thus, the city was taken. A total of *twenty-seven thousand men* may have been killed in the siege and after the city fell.

Verses 30-34: Benhadad humbles himself before Ahab. *Sackcloth* is a roughly woven, coarse garment that is worn as a sign of humiliation, slavery, or mourning. The exact meaning of *ropes upon our heads* is not known, but it is a sign of captivity and loss of power.

Ahab refers to Benhadad as his *brother* as was common among kings in ancient times (see, for example, 1 Kings 9:13). In the peace treaty, Ahab gets back some territory and gains trade advantages from the Syrians.

Verses 35-43: These verses condemn Ahab for not following the rules of the Holy War (see Deuteronomy 20:10-18) and killing Benhadad. People or things may be devoted to destruction (verse 42), that is, set aside for destruction. This is done to eliminate undesirable or dangerous elements from the community.

The unnamed prophet here has the same zeal for destroying pagans as does Elijah (see 1 Kings 18:40). The text does not report that God sent word to Ahab to kill Benhadad, but perhaps the prophet believes that Ahab should have understood this without being told.

Naboth's Vineyard (21:1-29)

This story shows how Jezebel continues to exert control over affairs in Israel and how Ahab refuses to uphold the covenant laws by which he and all Israel are supposed to live. Elijah speaks out to condemn the king and queen.

Verses 1-7: Naboth is a law-abiding Israelite who refuses to illegally give up the land that is his inheritance. According to covenant law, all land belongs to God, who graciously allows the people of Israel to use it. The land is the people's inheritance from God, and property is to remain in the family to which it is given (see Leviticus 25:13-34; also Numbers 27:1-11; Ezekiel 45:8).

Verses 8-16: Jezebel arranges to have Naboth falsely accused of cursing God, which carries the death penalty (see Exodus 22:28; Leviticus 24:16; Deuteronomy 17:5-6). Either the elders and nobles know what Jezebel is trying to do and go along with the plot (perhaps out of fear of the queen), or they are tricked into believing the false witnesses. The description of the two witnesses as *scoundrels* may have been left out of the official communication between the queen and the community officials.

According to 2 Kings 9:26, Naboth's sons are also killed. This would be necessary to keep them from avenging his wrongful death and from inheriting his property. Property for which there are no legal heirs goes to the king.

Verses 17-29: Verse 17 may mean that Elijah is to meet Ahab, who is (lives) in Samaria, in Naboth's vineyard in Jezreel. Elijah brings an oracle of punishment to Ahab for the murder of Naboth and the illegal appropriation of his property. Though Ahab did not directly order Naboth's death, he is willing to profit from it. Both he and Jezebel will give their lives in forfeit for the crime.

The writers of Kings also condemn Ahab for worshiping idols (verses 25-26).

Ahab repents of his evil ways and goes into a ritual of mourning to show his sincerity. This is a sign to God that the king now recognizes his proper place in relation to God and is willing to be obedient to God's laws.

Unlike Jezebel, who tries to kill Elijah, Ahab accepts

the prophet's role as one who may speak God's word of judgment and condemnation against the king's actions. Thus, the promised judgment is postponed to the next generation in Ahab's family. Ahaziah, however, does enough evil in his own right to warrant punishment even without the judgment carried over from his father's sins (see 1 Kings 22:51-53).

Ahab, Jehoshaphat, and Ahaziah (22:1-53)

This chapter picks up the story from Chapter 20 of Israel's wars with Syria. During the three years of peace between Israel and Syria, the two nations form a coalition with other relatively weak powers (including Hamath and possibly Egypt) to meet the rising threat from Assyria. King Shalmaneser III (859-825 B.C.) of Assyria leads his forces westward across the Euphrates River and then south through Syria toward Israel. The coalition forces meet his army at Qarqar in 853 B.C. Though the Assyrians later boast of a great victory, apparently the smaller nations are successful in stopping his drive.

Ahab's War Against Syria (22:1-40)

Verses 1-4: Ahab makes peace with Judah and marries his daughter to the son of Jehoshaphat (see 2 Kings 8:16-18). Ahab is apparently the dominant partner in the alliance. He then moves to take Ramoth-gilead from the Syrians who had taken the city in the days of Omri and have failed to give it back as Benhadad had promised (see 1 Kings 20:34).

Verses 5-12: Ahab wants God's instructions concerning the battle as did King David concerning the Philistines (see 1 Samuel 23:1-2). Ahab asks the prophets to mediate between him and God in this matter (see also Ezekiel 20:1). These prophets may be associated with the royal court as official advisors to the king.

Jehoshaphat is suspicious of their unanimously favorable opinion, despite Zedekiah's sign action demonstrating Israel's victory (verse 11). Micaiah is summoned and the kings wait for him at the traditional place for judging legal cases by the city gate.

Verses 13-23: Ahab must suspect that God is against him in this venture. He presses Micaiah to tell him the truth. Micaiah tells the kings of a vision (verse 17), and then delivers his oracle of judgment which also comes to him in a vision (verses 19-23).

The fact that God and the prophet have *spoken evil* (that is, have spoken words of judgment and punishment) begins the process of carrying out that evil. However, God is giving Ahab a chance to discern the *lying spirit* and to listen to the true prophetic word spoken by Micaiah (see also Deuteronomy 13:1-5 where God is said to test the people through false prophets).

Verses 24-36: Zedekiah cannot understand by what authority Micaiah speaks. Micaiah is content to let God prove that what he says is true.

Despite his suspicion of the truth, Ahab goes into battle. His plan to let Jehoshaphat take the more dangerous position and be a scapegoat does not work. Ahab cannot get around the will of God. He dies and leaves the army of Israel to retreat.

Verses 37-40: The report in verse 38 is related to Elijah's prophecy in 1 Kings 21:19, although Naboth died in Jezreel rather than in Samaria. Perhaps Naboth was stoned at an area outside the walls of Jezreel, near a pool that is like the pool near Samaria where Ahab's blood is washed from his chariot.

The ivory house that Ahab built may have contained ivory decorations such as have been found by archaeologists in the ruins of Samaria.

Jehoshaphat and Ahaziah (22:41-53)

Verses 41-50: Jehoshaphat is a faithful worshiper of God as was his father (see 1 Kings 15:9-15). He gets rid of the remaining prostitutes associated with fertility cults in

Judah, though he does not completely stop pagan worship services on the high places.

Jehoshaphat controls enough of Edom to try to revive Solomon's merchant fleet operations at Ezion-geber (see 1 Kings 9:26-28). He tries perhaps twice, once with Ahaziah (see 2 Chronicles 20:35-37) and once without him, but his plans fail.

According to 2 Chronicles 19:4-11, Jehoshaphat reforms the judicial system in Judah in order to have justice more uniformly administered within the country and to provide a system by which disputed cases can be appealed.

Verses 51-53: Ahaziah is a true son of Ahab and Jezebel. His short reign fulfills Elijah's prophecy to Ahab in 1 Kings 21:29.

§ § § § § § §

The Message of 1 Kings 20–22

The historical record of the books of Kings is history with a purpose; it is history told within the context of faith. The people who wrote Kings based their historical record on the belief that the creative will of God is behind all reality. Thus, events in history are not random or irrational but are related to the will and purposes of God.

Part of God's will is to be known by people (see, for example, 1 Kings 20:13, 28). What is knowledge of God, according to the Old Testament?

§ Knowledge is not only mental understanding but also involves the heart (as the source of a person's character) and the will (as the means of action in daily life).

§ One of the goals of human life is to know what God is like and what God requires.

§ People may know God through God's activities in the world and through God's relationships with individuals.

§ People may know God through God's word spoken by a prophet.

§ Knowledge of God requires understanding and practice of God's will.

§ Knowledge of God includes an active recognition and acknowledgment of God's power, grace, and claim on human devotion.

§ § § § § § §

2 Kings 1–3

Introduction to These Chapters

Second Kings picks up where First Kings left off in the reign of Ahaziah of Israel. Chapter 1 tells of Ahaziah's premature death, chapter 2 tells how Elisha takes over Elijah's prophetic ministry, and chapter 3 reports on Israel's and Judah's war with Moab.

Here is an outline of these chapters.
  I.   The Reign of Ahaziah (1:1-18)
 II.   Elisha Succeeds Elijah (2:1-25)
III.   The Reign of Jehoram (Joram) of Israel (3:1-27)

The Reign of Ahaziah (1:1-18)

Verses 1-8: Verse 1 is perhaps misplaced from 2 Kings 3, which tells about Israel's conflict with Moab. It is possible that Moab first withheld tribute from its Israelite overlords during Ahaziah's reign, but, because his reign was so short, it was left to his brother, Jehoram, to try to get Moab back under Israelite control.

Ahaziah shows his disloyalty to God by seeking an oracle from the Syrian god Baalzebub. This god's real name is Baalzebul, which means *baal the prince*. The Israelite historians have changed his name to Baalzebub, which means *lord of flies*, to mock this pagan god and his worshipers. Later, the name Baalzebub comes to be a synonym for Satan (see, for example, Matthew 12:24).

Because Ahaziah trusts in false gods rather than the one true God, he will die.

Elijah's clothing is a sign of his prophetic office. These rough clothes may also be a symbol of austerity and of Israel's former nomadic life, in contrast to the settled, more luxurious, and perhaps less faithful present life.

Verses 9-18: The soldiers perhaps are sent to bring Elijah to the king so the king may shut him up. Even though the first two captains greet Elijah as *man of God*, the prophet calls down God's fire of judgment upon them. The third captain humbles himself before Elijah and before God and so is spared.

Elijah repeats his oracle of judgment (*because . . . therefore*, verse 16) in front of the king. Thus, Ahaziah dies not only because of the sins of his father Ahab (see 1 Kings 21:29), but also because of his own sin in not being faithful to God.

Elisha Succeeds Elijah (2:1-25)

Elisha stays with Elijah, his master, until the very end and seeks to take on the responsibilities of Elijah's prophetic ministry.

Verses 1-5: Both Elijah and Elisha know that God will soon take Elijah away. Elisha refuses to obey Elijah's request to let him go on alone to meet his fate.

The *company of the prophets* is a group of prophets whose leaders are referred to as fathers and who are associated with various places or sanctuaries in Israel, here at Bethel (verse 3) and Jericho (verse 5; see also 1 Samuel 10:5).

Verses 6-14: Elijah asks Elisha three times to leave him (verses 2, 4, and 6), perhaps as a test of Elisha's determination and loyalty.

The fifty prophets from Jericho are witnesses to the parting of the water by Elijah's mantle, both by Elijah (verse 8) and by Elisha (verse 14). They see that the power to work wonders is transferred from Elijah to

Elisha and testify that Elisha has received the prophetic spirit (verse 15).

In Israelite families, the firstborn son is to receive a double portion of everything belonging to his father (see Deuteronomy 21:17). Elisha requests such a double inheritance of the prophetic spirit from his spiritual father, Elijah. Before he can inherit such a gift, however, he must pass one more test. If he can see Elijah being taken up into heaven, then he will be so blessed. Elisha must show his ability to see and understand the spiritual world. He must have visionary abilities which show that he will be open to the spirit of inspiration from God.

A storm wind and fire are often associated with God's appearing on earth. Elisha cries out (verse 12), both in astonishment and to show that he does indeed see what is ordinarily not seen by mortals. He tears his clothes as a sign of mourning for Elijah.

Elisha parting the waters of the Jordan shows that he has inherited Elijah's spiritual powers as well as his mantle. As he strikes the water, he calls on God to be present in the act and, thus, to manifest God's holy power through him.

Verses 15-18: The fifty prophets testify to Elisha's power, but they do not believe that Elijah is really gone (perhaps since Elijah had disappeared and reappeared before; see 1 Kings 17:1-9; 19:1-9).

Elisha is now their acknowledged leader, so they press him for permission to search for Elijah. *Until he was ashamed* (verse 17) may perhaps mean *for a long time* or *beyond measure.*

Verses 19-22: The leaders of Jericho seek Elisha's help in purifying a spring that is believed to be causing the land to not produce food and the people to not produce offspring. Modern research has suggested that some springs in this area can cause sterility because the water comes in contact with radioactive rocks underground.

The finest spring in Jericho is now called Elisha's Fountain.

Elisha uses salt in a purifying ritual to cancel the effects of Joshua's curse against Jericho (see Joshua 6:26) on this particular spring.

Verses 23-25: This incident, like that of the previous verses, testifies to Elisha's authority as a prophet and as a man who can work wonders. Though the story is told perhaps to insure respect for prophets and their powers, calling down a curse on children because of their rudeness does seem (from our present point of view anyway) cruel and unjust.

Israelites are forbidden to shave their heads (see Deuteronomy 14:1-2). The boys treat Elisha's baldness as a mark of shame, though some scholars say that prophets would sometimes shave their heads as symbols of their office. *Forty-two* is perhaps a number symbolic of ill-omen (see also 2 Kings 10:14; Revelation 11:2).

The Reign of Jehoram (Joram) of Israel (3:1-27)

Israel, Judah, and Edom fall back from their battle with Moab even though Elisha promises them victory.

Verses 1-3: The *eighteenth year of Jehoshaphat* does not agree with 2 Kings 1:17, which says that Jehoram of Israel became king in the second year of Jehoram of Judah. The two sources used by the writers of Kings for these texts must have used different systems of dating the reigns of the kings of Judah and Israel (see Introduction to First and Second Kings, "The Chronology of First and Second Kings"). Jehoram of Israel attempts some religious reform and is not as unfaithful to God as his parents were. He does not, however, win unqualified approval from the historians. He perhaps tolerates or even participates in worship at high places, as did Jeroboam (see 1 Kings 13:33-34) and Solomon (see 1 Kings 11:5-8).

Verses 4-8: A black basalt monument called the Moabite Stone was found by archaeologists in the 1860s.

The stone has an inscription that tells of Israel's war with Moab from the perspective of King Mesha of Moab. It celebrates his victory, which he attributes to his god Chemosh.

At this time, Israel is stronger than Judah and Edom is still under Judah's control, so the king of Israel can command their help against Moab.

Verses 9-20: The coalition plans to attack Moab from the south after marching around the Dead Sea through Edom. They expect to find water in the border area next to Moab, but they do not.

Apparently Elisha has been traveling with the army. He is identified as Elijah's servant (verse 11) and as a prophet (verse 12). Elisha wants to have nothing to do with Jehoram, who still associates with the pagan prophets of Ahab and Jezebel. He agrees to seek a word from God for the kings, however, because of his respect for Jehoshaphat (verse 14). He also wants to prove that God did not deceive the kings into coming to their destruction in Moab (verse 13).

Music is sometimes used to help put a prophet into a receptive state for a message from God (see also 1 Samuel 10:5-6). Elisha's message is that God will send water at dawn so that the attackers will be able to conquer the Moabites. They will be able to ruin the country.

Verses 21-27: The red sandstone that is characteristic of this area colors the water red in the rising sun and thus fools the Moabites.

The forces of Israel, Judah, and Edom have victory within their grasp until Mesha takes a desperate measure. The king sacrifices his eldest son to his god Chemosh in order to rouse the god to save the nation.

From the Moabite side, they believe that the wrath of Chemosh saves them from the Israelites. The Moabite Stone gives Chemosh credit for the victory.

From the Israelite/Judean side, they may lose their faith in God and panic at the thought of this local god's wrath when they realize that Mesha has taken such a desperate measure to save the city.

§ § § § § § §

The Message of 2 Kings 1–3

Elisha inherits Elijah's prophetic spirit and begins his own prophetic ministry after Elijah is carried away into heaven. This prophetic spirit is a portion of God's spirit that is granted to them. This spirit is a sign of their authority as prophets and the true substance of their ministries. They are vessels for the communication of God's spirit on earth. What does the Old Testament tell us about God's spirit?

§ God's spirit is a creative, life-giving, and personal force.

§ This spirit expresses God's nature and presence. It is a means by which God's nature is communicated to human beings.

§ God's spirit expresses both God's will and God's work to accomplish the divine purposes in the world.

§ The spirit of God is evident in the actions of human history.

§ This spirit is granted by God to those who are receptive and who are called by God for a special task.

§ To be filled with the spirit of the Lord is to have a divine gift for leadership as well as extraordinary insight.

§ God gives such a gift not only to the prophets but also to other charismatic leaders among God's people (for example, Gideon, David, and Saul).

§ God's spirit also works in and through ordinary people for the inspiration and perfection of the community of faith.

§ Both God's immediate and ultimate purposes for the world are accomplished through the ones who possess this gift.

§ § § § § § §

2 Kings 4–7

Introduction to These Chapters

These chapters contain stories about the wonders
worked by the prophet Elisha both in the lives of
individuals and in the political and military world. These
stories testify to Elisha's power and authority as a
prophet. They may be outlined as follows.

The Widow's Jar of Oil (4:1-7)

This woman's husband had been a member of a group
of prophets who look to Elisha as their spiritual leader.
Despite his faithfulness to God, the man went into debt
that his widow is unable to repay. She is faced with the
prospect of giving her children to the creditor, who will
sell them as slaves to collect his money or use them as his
personal slaves in exchange for cancelling the debt.

Selling children into slavery is allowed in Israelite law
(see Exodus 21:7). Though this law was later modified to
limit the term of service required (see Leviticus 25:39-46;
Deuteronomy 15:12-18), there were those among the

people of Israel who abused this right and took advantage of their fellow Israelites for their own gain (see, for example, Nehemiah 5:4-8; Jeremiah 34:8-16; Amos 2:6).

The woman acts in faith to obey Elisha's instructions, and the quantity of oil she receives is limited only by the number of vessels she is able to collect.

The Shunammite's Son Is Raised (4:8-37)

A wealthy woman who offers hospitality to Elisha is rewarded with the birth of a son. After the son's death, Elisha restores the child to life and demonstrates the extraordinary powers that he possesses as a "man of God."

Verses 1-17: This woman has wealth, she is the mistress of her household, she has a family who offers her security and protection in time of need, her husband is still living, and she has a faith in God that is expressed in her recognition of and hospitality to Elisha. The one thing missing in her life is a son. The people of Israel believe that children are a blessing from God and are a sign of God's favor. To be childless is a great tragedy.

Despite her initial doubts about Elisha's promise, she does bear a son.

Verses 18-31: When the son dies, apparently of a sunstroke, the woman immediately goes to Elisha to confront him with the tragedy.

Her husband may not realize that the child is dead because he questions her trip to see Elisha. The first day of the *new moon* and the *sabbath* are both days of rest, and are perhaps considered as the best or most appropriate times to consult with a prophet. The woman replies with the single word *Shalom*, which in this case has the general meaning of "Everything will be all right."

As she humbles herself at the prophet's feet, she reveals the tragedy to Elisha, who has had no warning about all this from God. The woman is in *bitter distress* over the loss of her child, especially because she did not ask for the child but was freely promised him by Elisha. She thus feels that Elisha (and God) have been deceitful to promise her a son and then to allow him to die.

Elisha instructs his servant to carry the prophet's staff, which is a symbol of his power, and put it on the child. The servant is to speak to no one on the way so that he will not delay and so that the power he is carrying from Elisha will not be diminished. The mother trusts only in Elisha's presence, however, so they follow Gehazi.

Verses 32-37: Elisha's resuscitation of the child is similar to that performed by Elijah in 1 Kings 17:17-24. Elisha's God-given power allows him to transfer the life-force from his body into the child's. The seven sneezes are evidence that the breath of life has returned to the boy.

Elisha and the Pot of Death (4:38-41)

This incident may take place during the seven-year famine spoken of in 2 Kings 8:1. The prophets are reduced to seeking uncultivated food perhaps because of the food shortage.

The poison gourd may be the colocynth, which could be mistaken for a gourd cucumber and which is poisonous. Elisha counteracts the poisonous effects of the gourd by throwing in wholesome meal, and through his abilities as a man of God who can bring life out of death.

The Abundance of Loaves and Grain (4:42-44)

This story shows that prophets are supported, in part, by gifts from the people.

Bread of the first fruits (NRSV) is bread made from the *first ripe grain* (NIV) milled during the harvest season. *First fruits* are offerings made to God from the bounty of the land. The *ears* or *heads of grain* are perhaps ears of corn. By acting in faith on Elisha's word, the servant is able to feed all the prophets (as in 4:1-7; see also Matthew 14:13-21).

This story shows that the *word of the Lord* can provide the basic necessities of life as well as affect the destinies of nations (as in 2 Kings 6:15-23).

Naaman's Leprosy Is Cured (5:1-27)

The faith, cure, and confession of this Syrian commander show God's concern for all people and the availability of healing and righteousness even to those who are not born into the community of faith.

Verses 1-7: Naaman's skill as a warrior and his position of favor in Syria are attributed to the fact that God has used him to give Syria victories, perhaps over Israel as punishment for sin (see, for example, 1 Kings 22:13-36; also Jeremiah 25:1-9).

The Hebrew term that is translated *leprosy* refers to a wide range of skin diseases, some of which are what is called leprosy today (see Leviticus 13 on the diagnosis of these diseases). Naaman may have had a disease other than true leprosy, since he has access to the king of Syria and is not in isolation.

Naaman goes to the king of Israel thinking that he, as the most powerful man in Israel, will have the power to cure him. This incident cannot be dated exactly, because neither the Syrian nor the Israelite king involved are named.

The value of the silver and gold that Naaman offers for a cure has been estimated at $80,000.

Verses 8-14: Naaman is enraged because Elisha will not personally come to him and heal him in a public ceremony. He has preconceived ideas about what is appropriate in this situation and follows Elisha's instructions only after his servants reason with him. The cleansing action of the water combines with the faith he shows by doing as he is told, and he is cured.

Verses 15-19: Naaman now sees Elisha face to face and

offers him, as the representative of God, the reward for healing him. Since, as God's servant, Elisha will not accept payment for the cure, Naaman offers to be a faithful worshiper of God back in his own country. To do this, he asks for soil from Israel. Behind this request is the belief that the god of a nation or region is most powerful or is closer to worshipers on home territory (see also Psalm 137:4).

Naaman also asks forgiveness for having to go with the Syrian king into the temple of Rimmon, the Syrian god, and participate in worship there as part of his duties to the king. Elisha forgives him on God's behalf and blesses him.

Verses 19-27: This related story shows that deceit and greed do not go unnoticed nor unpunished by God. Gehazi gets money from Naaman apparently so he can buy property, livestock, and servants (verse 26), and raise his standard of living above that of a prophet's servant. Because of his sin, he and his family are cursed with leprosy.

Elisha and the Floating Axe-Head (6:1-7)

This is another one of the wonder stories told about Elisha that witness to his power and authority as a prophet. The rescue of a lost axe-head shows how the prophets and those who recorded these stories found evidence of God's activity even in the most commonplace events in their lives.

Elisha Saved from the Syrian Army (6:8-23)

The details of this story show Elisha's extraordinary psychic skills in knowing the military plans of the enemy and in seeing what others cannot see.

Verses 8-14: With the help of Elisha's knowledge of the Syrian army's plans, the king of Israel can avoid a confrontation with them. Elisha's fame, however, spreads to the Syrians, who set out to capture him.

The date of this incident is not known, because the story does not identify the kings involved. Clearly, however, this takes place during a time when Syria is stronger than Israel, because Syrian forces are free to encamp around Dothan, which is only ten miles north of Israel's capital city, Samaria.

Verses 15-23: That Elisha can see the divine horses and chariots of fire that are not visible to others is testimony to his receptive spirit (as in 2 Kings 2:9-12). The Syrians and the Israelites cannot see the help that God has sent Elisha. Now the prophet prays that the Syrians will be made literally blind so that he may go out to them and lead them into Samaria.

That God answers Elisha's prayer is a demonstration of his spiritual power and his close standing with God.

My father (verse 21) is a title of respect that the king uses toward Elisha. Elisha shows compassion on the captured soldiers by not calling down the chariots of fire upon them and by not allowing the king of Israel to kill them. To take captives *with your sword and with your bow* (verse 22) may refer to soldiers who surrendered and who should not be executed in cold blood.

Either because of their kind treatment by the Israelites or because of their fear of Israel's powerful God, the Syrians send no more raiding parties into Israel, at least for a while.

Syrian Siege of Samaria (6:24–7:20)

Sometime after the incidents of the previous verses the Syrians attack Israel. Elisha's spiritual and psychic powers once again save his life, and he delivers God's word concerning the fate of Samaria.

Verses 24-31: There was more than one Syrian king named Ben-hadad, so this siege cannot be dated precisely. The Israelite king in this instance may be Jehoahaz or perhaps his son, Jehoash.

The Samaritans have endured a long siege and food is running out in the city. Terrible food is being sold for very high prices, and some people have even resorted to cannibalism. Cannibalism is among the curses listed in Deuteronomy 28 that are brought on by disobedience to God (see Deuteronomy 28:54-57).

The king is extremely distressed by this, even to the point of tearing his clothes and wearing sackcloth, which are signs of mourning. He blames God (verse 33) and Elisha, as God's representative, for the awful condition of the city and its people. Perhaps Elisha had announced the coming of the siege or had spoken about it as punishment from God for Israel's sins.

The king is determined to get rid of Elisha as the spokesman for a God who, in the king's view anyway, would bring such a tragedy on the chosen people.

Verses 32–7:2: The king confronts the prophet with his belief that God has visited this suffering on the people. He demands to know why he should patiently wait any longer for anything good to come from God: What more can I hope for from the Lord?

Elisha responds with an oracle from God. He announces that the next day good food will once again be available in Samaria's marketplace, though at a high price.

Verses 3-15: By divine providence, four lepers, who feel they have nothing to lose by approaching the enemy, go in search of food among the Syrians. They discover that God has tricked the Syrians into fleeing and leaving behind all their provisions (verses 6-7).

The four men realize that they must not keep the good news—nor the bounty of the Syrian camp—to themselves. They are obligated to share the good news with their fellow Israelites.

The king is suspicious of their deliverance from the Syrians, despite Elisha's prophecy of the day before. He must have the word of his messengers as well.

Verses 16-20: Elisha's words are fulfilled concerning the food and the fate of the king's captain.

FIRST AND SECOND KINGS

§ § § § § § §

The Message of 2 Kings 4–7

§ The stories in these chapters about wonders worked by Elisha fulfill different purposes as Scripture. They are, first of all, dramatic and entertaining narratives. They also testify to Elisha's power and authority as a prophet. Working wonders is not, in and of itself, however, the mark of a true prophet (see, for example, Deuteronomy 13:1-5). What qualities distinguish a true prophet from a false one?

§ True prophets wait on God's word and do not proclaim their limited human imaginings (see Jeremiah 23:21; Ezekiel 13:3).

§ True prophets are receptive to the visible world and the (normally) invisible world of God's reality (see 2 Kings 6:15-17).

§ True prophets are watchmen among the people of Israel who guard the covenant and who raise an alarm when Israel's faith falls short of the covenant (see Ezekiel 3:16-21).

§ The wonders and signs that true prophets perform promote faith and are in the service of life among God's people (see 2 Kings 4:1-7). Their words *do good to one who walks uprightly* (NRSV) or, as rendered in the NIV, *do good to him whose ways are upright* (see Micah 2:7).

§ True prophets do not accept money for favorable messages (see 2 Kings 5).

§ True prophets announce God's word of punishment as well as of salvation (see Isaiah 10:20-27).

§ True prophets are ethically and spiritually righteous in their personal lives (see Micah 3:5-8).

§ The word of a true prophet is confirmed by God, though perhaps not immediately (see Ezekiel 12:21-25).

§ § § § § § §

PART ELEVEN 2 Kings 8–10

Introduction to These Chapters

Chapters 8–10 tell about the end of the house of Ahab in Israel and the establishment of the house of Jehu. The prophet Elisha plays a key role in bringing about Jehu's revolution and in bringing a change of rulers in Syria. The historians of Kings regard all these events as fulfillment of earlier prophecies that condemn the family of Ahab and promise its extinction. These prophecies are fulfilled, however, at a terrible cost to the nation both in terms of lives and leadership lost and in terms of political and military stability lost.

These chapters may be outlined as follows.
  I. Elisha, Hazael, and Jehoram (8:1-24)
     A. Elisha and the Shunammite Woman (8:1-6)
     B. Elisha and the Revolt of Hazael in Syria (8:7-15)
     C. The Reign of Jehoram (Joram) in Judah (8:16-24)
 II. Ahaziah Reigns, Jehu Revolts (8:25–9:29)
III. The Death of Jezebel (9:30-37)
 IV. The Reign of Jehu (10:1-36)

Elisha, Hazael, and Jehoram (8:1-24)

This chapter tells about another wonder worked by Elisha, and then moves on to deal with the political and military changes going on in Syria and Israel. Elisha is a catalyst for change in both nations.

Elisha and the Shunammite Woman (8:1-6)

This is the woman whose son Elisha restored to life (see 2 Kings 4:8-37). In times past Israelites have journeyed to Philistia (see Genesis 26:1) and to Egypt (see Genesis 42:1-2) to survive a famine in their own land. The famine in this case is one sent by God, perhaps for sins of the people of Israel that are not named here (as the drought of 1 Kings 17 comes from God).

While the woman is away, her property is taken over by the state and is held in trust for her though the land is still used in her absence. It is customary to restore property after seven years to its original owners, who may have lost control of their land because of absence or debt.

This incident must take place before Gehazi is stricken with leprosy (see 2 Kings 5:20-27), or else he is suffering from a form of the disease that does not require him to be isolated from other people. As in many of these stories about Elisha, the king involved is not named.

The woman receives not only her land but also the income which was made from the property while she was gone.

Elisha and the Revolt of Hazael in Syria (8:7-15)

Elisha now moves to carry out one of three commands which God gave Elijah at Mount Horeb (see 1 Kings 19:15-16). Elijah had only carried out one of the commands, which was to anoint Elisha as his disciple and successor. As an outside power, Syria has been divinely ordained to punish the house of Ahab and those people in Israel who have worshiped idols.

When Hazael comes to consult with Elisha on the king's behalf, Elisha tells him the whole truth of the matter but instructs him not to tell the king everything. Elisha's message is that the king certainly would or could recover from his disease if he were to live long enough, but the king will die before getting well.

Another possible translation for verse 11 is "The man of God kept his face expressionless for a long time; and then he wept." Elisha is visualizing the horrors the people of Israel will suffer because of their sin. He knows that the punishment is God's will, but he grieves for his people.

Hazael is not at all horrified about what Elisha says will happen. He is just amazed that he of all people should be chosen to accomplish such glorious deeds. Hazael then proceeds to carry out Elisha's prophecy (verse 13) by smothering Ben-hadad on his sickbed and by taking the throne for himself.

The Reign of Jehoram (Joram) of Judah (8:16-24)

Jehoram is sometimes called Joram (verse 21) like his brother-in-law, the king of Israel.

Joram's wife is Athaliah, who is the daughter of King Ahab and Queen Jezebel. Joram is condemned by the writers of Kings for following his wife's family in idol worship, perhaps after Athaliah introduces the worship of Baal-Melqart into the city of Jerusalem. According to 2 Chronicles 21:2-4, Joram kills all his brothers and their supporters in order to eliminate any possible rivals to the throne.

In spite of Jehoram's sins, God chooses not to destroy Judah because of past promises that the house of David would always be on the throne in Jerusalem (see, for example, 1 Kings 11:36). The *lamp* is a symbol for life and for the permanence of David's line.

Judah does lose some territory during Jehoram's reign, however. The loss of the Philistine city of Libnah is not a great blow, but it does show the difficulty Jehoram has in controlling his frontiers. The loss of sway over Edom has more serious consequences. This means that Judah loses its seaport and fortress at Ezion-geber and its access to southern trading routes to Arabia, which is bad for the Judean economy.

Ahaziah Reigns, Jehu Revolts (8:25-9:29)

Ahaziah reigns only one year in Judah before he is caught up in the revolution going on in Israel and is killed. He is condemned by the historians of Kings for following in the tradition of the house of Ahab, who was his grandfather on his mother's side. This must mean that he worshiped idols as his mother and father did, instead of being faithful to God (see also 2 Chronicles 22:1-9).

Israel is still struggling with the Syrians at Ramoth-gilead (sometimes called Ramah) in the conflict begun by Ahab (see 1 Kings 22). The stage is set for Ahaziah's death when he goes to visit Jehoram at Jezreel during this conflict.

Verses 1-13: Elisha appoints one of his followers to carry out the last of the three commissions God gave Elijah (see 1 Kings 19:15-18). The young man is to anoint Jehu as Samuel anointed Saul and David (see 1 Samuel 10:1; 16:13).

This anointing will legitimize Jehu's claim to the throne. As has been said earlier, the Northern Kingdom does not have a strong tradition for a king's son to automatically follow him in office. There is still support here for the tradition that a king is named by divine designation by a prophet and by public acclamation (see the discussion on 1 Kings 1:1–2:46).

Verses 7-10a elaborate on Elisha's original instructions to the young man about what he is to say as he anoints Jehu (see verse 3). The elaboration may come from one of the historians who bases this speech on prophecies concerning Ahab and Jezebel found in 1 Kings 17–19 and 1 Kings 21:23.

Jehu's fellow officers speak of the young prophet as a *mad man* (verse 11), perhaps thinking that, as a prophet, he must be given to fits of ecstasy. They are, however, willing to accept the prophet's designation of Jehu as Israel's new king.

Verses 14-29: With great cunning Jehu carries out the

assassinations of Joram and Ahaziah. The two kings think that Jehu brings news of the battle with the Syrians at Ramoth-gilead. Joram asks if the fighting is over, bringing peace and victory to Israel (verse 22). Jehu answers the question in the larger context of peace, or well-being, for Israel as a whole. Israel cannot enjoy true peace until the evils of pagan religion are gone.

The deaths of Joram (Ahab's son) and Ahaziah (Ahab's grandson) begin to carry out the prophecies against Ahab made by Elijah (see 1 Kings 21:17-19, 28-29).

Verse 29 may be a correction of 2 Kings 8:25 added by a later editor of Kings, or it could be a date for Ahaziah's reign that is made under a different system of dating from that used in 8:25.

The Death of Jezebel (9:30-37)

Jezebel knows what Jehu has done and knows she is going to die. She boldly greets him and accuses him of being like Zimri who, despite his numerous political murders, was king for only a week (see 1 Kings 16:8-20).

Jehu decides that Jezebel deserves a proper burial since, after all, she was the daughter of a king. By this time, however, the prophecy concerning her in 1 Kings 21:23 has already been fulfilled.

The Reign of Jehu (10:1-36)

Jehu ruthlessly and efficiently kills all the males related to Ahab and kills those who support them. He has the worshipers of Baal in Israel massacred in order to cleanse the land of the idolatry and witchcraft of Jezebel (see 2 Kings 9:22).

Verses 1-11: Jehu justifies the murder of Ahab's descendants as fulfillment of the prophecies spoken by Elijah against Ahab's family (see 1 Kings 21:20-21). That nothing of the word of the LORD shall fall to the earth (verse 10) means that nothing that the Lord has spoken concerning the house of Ahab shall remain unfulfilled.

Jehu takes responsibility for killing Joram, but he absolves himself and the people of Samaria for the deaths of Ahab's sons and claims that, in reality, it is God who struck them down.

Verses 12-17: Relatives of Ahaziah from Judah who had been visiting in the north are killed as they travel back home (verses 12-14).

Jehu receives support in his campaign against Ahab's family from Jehonadab, who is a Rechabite. The Rechabites are a clan living in both Israel and Judah who are apparently related to the Kenites, a nomadic desert-dwelling people who allied themselves with the Israelites during the days of the Judges (see Judges 4–5; also Jeremiah 35:1-19).

The Rechabites live in tents instead of houses. They are shepherds, not farmers, and they refuse to drink wine. Their way of life supports their belief that Israel's true worship of God is found in her desert-dwelling days. They condemn the pagan practices that became part of Israel's settled, agricultural life in Canaan. Since grape culture and wine-making are not practiced by nomads, wine becomes a symbol to the Rechabites of the corruptions found in settled life in Canaan. The Rechabites are, thus, natural allies for Jehu in his efforts to rid Israel of pagan influences.

Verses 18-27: Jehu, like Elijah (see 1 Kings 18:40), slaughters the worshipers of Baal. He has the sacred objects of the Baal temple destroyed and turns the site of the temple into a latrine, as a continuing reminder to the people of the status of pagan cults in Israel and as a continuing insult to the memory of the idol worshipers.

The prophet Hosea later condemns Jehu for his excessive bloodshed (see Hosea 1:4-5).

Verses 28-36: Jehu gets rid of Baal worship, but keeps the golden calf shrines in Bethel and Dan that Jeroboam created (see 1 Kings 12:26-30). Though these shrines are related to the worship of God, they are looked upon as sinful and unlawful by the writers of Kings.

Jehu proves to be unable to hold onto Israelite territory east of the Jordan. The Syrian king Hazael takes advantage of the chaos within Israel and of the relatively weak power of Assyria at this time to extend his territory east of the Jordan to Moab. Assyria does, however, manage to command tribute from the kings of Tyre and Sidon and from Jehu.

The deaths of Ahaziah and Jezebel also break Israelite ties with Judah and Phoenicia. This leaves Israel not only confused internally but also surrounded by hostile powers.

§ § § § § § §

The Message of 2 Kings 8–10

Of all the persistent issues raised in the Scripture, perhaps none is more difficult to deal with than that of divinely-ordained bloodshed. The books of Kings have their fair share of prophetic proclamations (see, for example, 1 Kings 14:7-13; 2 Kings 8:10-13) and prophetic actions (see, for example, 1 Kings 18:40) that result in people's deaths. How are we to understand these events?

Some aspects of this issue are based on the belief that guilt or sin affects a whole social group, especially the family. The sin of one member contaminates the rest and makes them a potential source of evil which must be eliminated (see, for example, the laws of Exodus 20:5 and Deuteronomy 5:9-10, and their application in Numbers 16:31-33, Joshua 7:24-25, 2 Samuel 21:3-9, and 1 Kings 21:21).

Such vengeance is also based on the belief that God is righteous and just and that God will maintain righteousness and justice within human history. Sin will be punished and wrongs set right.

This is not, however, the only word on how sin and wrongdoing are handled in the community of faith (see, for example, Deuteronomy 24:16; 2 Kings 14:6; also Jeremiah 23; 31:29-30; Ezekiel 13; 14:9; 18:2-4). These other laws and prophetic oracles uphold individual rather than corporate responsibility for wrongdoing.

Scripture also shows us that even those who are divinely ordained for leadership must live under the law and are subject to condemnation for taking judgment too far. The prophet Hosea, for example, condemns the brutality and bloodshed of Jehu's reign (see 1 Kings 19:15-17; 2 Kings 9–10; Hosea 1:4). Though designated king of Israel by God, Jehu goes too far in his zeal to secure the throne and to eliminate any opposition to his rule. In this case we may say that God's will ordained the change of leadership in Israel, but that human free will unfortunately made the suffering of innocent people a part of the change (see also 2 Kings 8:10-13).

From our present perspective, we may acknowledge the element of human free will at work in both the good things and the terrible things that happen in human history. Though history is moving toward God's ultimately redemptive ends, the innocent and the guilty alike still suffer. We may also acknowledge that we have the benefit of God's revelation in Jesus Christ, who teaches that we are to love our enemies and pray for those who abuse us (see Luke 6:27-31), and that we are each responsible before God for our lives (see Luke 16:19-31).

§ § § § § § §

Introduction to These Chapters

These chapters cover the reigns of Athaliah, Jehoash, and Amaziah in Judah and Jehoahaz, Jehoash, and Jeroboam II in Israel. They may be outlined as follows.
  I. The Reign of Queen Athaliah (11:1-21)
 II. The Reign of Jehoash (Joash) in Judah (12:1-21)
III. The Reign of Jehoahaz (13:1-9)
IV. The Reign of Joash (Jehoash) in Israel (13:10-25)
 V. The Reign of Amaziah (14:1-22)
VI. The Reign of Jeroboam II (14:23-29)

The Reign of Queen Athaliah (11:1-21)

After King Ahaziah of Judah is killed by Jehu in Israel (see 2 Kings 9:27-28), his mother Athaliah seizes the throne in Jerusalem. Despite her efficiency in killing her rivals to the throne, however, her reign is short.

Athaliah is the daughter of Ahab and Jezebel, and is not of the house of David. So she has no legitimate claim to the throne of Judah, which God had promised to David's family (see 1 Kings 11:36). She is also a strong supporter of the cult of Baal-Melqart, as was her mother. At this time, Judah is much more faithful to the worship of God than is Israel. There is less support for and participation in foreign cults, and so Athaliah has few religious sympathizers.

After six years, Athaliah is killed and her grandson, Joash, is crowned king.

Verses 1-3: Jehosheba is the daughter of King Joram

but not of Athaliah. She is the half-sister of Ahaziah, and she hides Ahaziah's son, Joash, from his murderous grandmother. According to 2 Chronicles 22:11, she is the wife of Jehoiada, the priest who crowns Joash king and has Athaliah killed.

Verses 4-12: The Carites are mercenaries (perhaps from Crete) who are part of the royal bodyguard. Apparently one-third of the royal guard usually goes off duty in the Temple area on the sabbath to guard the palace. Jehoiada, however, instructs them all to remain in the Temple area so as to protect the young king and to leave the palace unprotected.

The *spears and shields* of King David may be ones that David dedicated for use in the Temple on royal occasions, or may be ones used by David himself that are then symbolically turned over to the new king.

The *crown* is probably made of gold and may be worn over a turban. The *covenant* is perhaps a copy of the responsibilities of and promises made by God and the people of Israel.

Verses 13-21: The *pillar* (verse 14) is probably one of the free-standing pillars at the entrance to the Temple (see 1 Kings 7:15-22).

There is a ceremonial reaffirmation of the covenant between God and the king (the covenant that God made with the house of David), between God and the people (the Sinai covenant), and between the king and the people (in which they promise to mutually support one another).

Because he is still a child, Jehoash (Joash) is guided by Jehoiada and perhaps also by Jehosheba, since his own mother is dead.

The Reign of Jehoash (Joash) in Judah (12:1-21)

This account speaks favorably of Joash and tells about his concern for the maintenance of the Temple. The parallel account of his reign in 2 Chronicles 24 reveals, however, that Joash forsakes God after the death of Jehoiada, the priest who was responsible for Joash becoming king (see 2 Chronicles 24:15-19). The king is faithful all the days in which Jehoiada instructs him or because of Jehoiada's guidance (verse 2).

Joash also has military problems with Syria and must pay heavy tribute to King Hazael in order to save Jerusalem from the Syrian army.

Verses 1-3: Joash is given credit for being *right* before God in spite of the fact that pagan worship practices continue in Judah. Worship *on the high places* is probably not the worship of Baal that was imported from Tyre by Jezebel in Israel and Athaliah in Judah (see 2 Kings 11:18-19). Such services are probably part of cults which are native to Judah and which were practiced first by the Canaanites and then picked up by the Israelites after their conquest of Canaan. These services may also be in high places that were established by King Solomon (see 1 Kings 3:2-3; 11:6-8).

Verses 4-16: Until this time the Temple had probably been maintained by the king out of the royal treasury. Joash moves to shift this burden of support to the priests and the people. He instructs the priests to take money to pay for the Temple repairs out of the funds they receive as their priestly allowance.

The priests receive income from taxes and from voluntary gifts (on the *assessment of persons* see Leviticus 27:2-8).

The priest's *treasurer* or benefactor is perhaps an official who aids in the collection of Temple revenues.

The priests fail in this new duty so the king arranges for his officials to collect the money and pay the workmen themselves. The workmen's honesty is in sharp contrast to the implied dishonesty of the priests. The priests are allowed to keep income from guilt and sin offerings (see Leviticus 5:15-16) which are payments made in compensation for wrongs done. Since it is given in payment for sin this money cannot be used to repair the holy building.

Verses 17-18: Hazael takes advantage of a respite from Assyrian aggression to move against both Israel (see 2 Kings 10:32-33) and Judah. Joash must empty his treasury and that of the Temple in order to save his capital. Hazael is probably more interested in controlling the main trade routes in Judah than in occupying Jerusalem.

The writers of Chronicles attribute this defeat to the fact that Joash is unfaithful to God (see 2 Chronicles 24:23-24).

Verses 19-21: The Chronicler also traces Joash's assassination to his idol worship. Because Joash turns his back on God after Jehoiada's death Zechariah, the priest's son, rebukes the king in an oracle from God. The king and other leaders of Judah conspire to kill Zechariah, and this leads to the king's death at the hands of his own servants (see 2 Chronicles 24:20-27).

Silla is perhaps a suburb of Jerusalem. On the *Millo* see the comments on 1 Kings 9:15.

The Reign of Jehoahaz (13:1-9)

The reign of Jehoahaz comes during a difficult time for Israel. Jehoahaz continues in the idol worship and perversion of the worship of God begun during the reign of Jeroboam I (see 1 Kings 12:25-33). Jehoahaz also tolerates the worship of the goddess Asherah and allows the objects of her worship to remain in Israel.

According to the writers of Kings, all this leads to Syria's continued oppression of Israel, which was begun in the reign of Jehu (see 2 Kings 8:7-13; 10:28-33). Jehoahaz's army is greatly reduced.

Israel is saved from complete destruction, however, because the king pleads with God for relief from Syrian oppression and, presumably, repents to some extent from his idol worship. God takes pity on the sufferings of the people and sends a savior or deliverer for Israel as in the days of the judges (see Judges 3:9, 15). This deliverer is not identified, but with the deliverer's help the people are given sufficient relief from the conflict with Syria so that they can go back to their homes and resume their normal lives.

The Israelites do not enjoy any real success against the Syrians until the reign of Joash, the son of Jehoahaz.

The Reign of Joash (Jehoash) in Israel (13:10-25)

Joash is said to follow in his ancestors' footsteps by worshiping idols and leading the people into idol worship and away from God (see 1 Kings 12:25-33; 13:1-2). He does have some military success against the Syrians, however, thanks to Elisha's deathbed prophecy, and also against the Judeans (see 2 Kings 14:11-14).

Verses 10-13: This brief account of Joash's reign is supplemented with other information in verses 14-25 and in 2 Kings 14:8-16.

Verse 14: Joash greets the dying Elisha as *father*, a term of respect and reverence (see also 2 Kings 6:21). This indicates that the king recognizes Elisha's authority as a prophet despite the fact that the king is said to do *evil* in God's sight (verse 11).

Joash also calls Elisha *the chariots of Israel and its horsemen*, which reflects the prophet's role in Israelite military victories (see, for example, 2 Kings 3:13-20; 6:8-12, 33; 7:15). Elisha has been a channel of God's power and words to Israel, both in victory and in punishment (see, for example 2 Kings 8:10-13).

Verses 15-19: Elisha's last recorded prophecy in Kings assures Israel of victories over Syria. He commands Joash to perform sign actions that demonstrate these victories.

In Old Testament prophecy, sign actions are demonstrations of God's word (see, for example, Jeremiah 19:1-13; Ezekiel 12:1-16). Sign actions, like prophetic messages, begin the process of carrying out the word of God. The prophetic future begins with the spoken word or the sign action (see also the discussion of prophetic speech in the comments on 1 Kings 14:1-20; 18:17-19).

Joash shoots the arrow eastward because the Israelites will fight the Syrians to the east of Samaria across the Jordan River.

The fact that Elisha does not tell the king how many times to strike the ground with the arrows seems to indicate that he is testing the king. Joash's forcefulness and determination (or lack of them) are demonstrated in his striking the ground only three times.

Verses 20-21: Elisha's bones are said to have the same power to raise the dead as Elisha had in life (see 2 Kings 4:32-35).

Military raids into Israel by Moabites, Ammonites, and Midianites from across the Jordan were common.

The *grave* is a tomb cut into a hillside in which more than one person is buried. The tomb here is probably Elisha's family tomb. In general, bodies are prepared for burial and then are left on a stone shelf or ledge until they decay and only the bones are left. If a tomb becomes crowded, bones may be collected and put into stone boxes so that room will be made for more burials in the tomb.

Verses 22-23: These verses are related to verses 4-6, which tell of Israel's relief from Syria. Though oppressed, Israel is not overwhelmed and does manage to win some victories over Syria.

Israel survives because of God's compassion and because God remains true to the covenant promises of the past (see Genesis 12:1-2; 17:21; 35:11-12). The writers of Kings make it clear that Israel does not survive on its own merit but only because of God's mercy and because God's will is for the people of Israel to remain in the covenant relationship.

These verses are probably written after the fall of

Israel to the Assyrians in 722 B.C. The writers know that Israel is saved until now (that is, until the days of Joash), but that the nation will eventually perish.

Verses 24-25: Joash recovers some Israelite territory lost to Syria as he achieves the three victories foretold by Elisha.

The Reign of Amaziah (14:1-22)

Chapter 14 tells of the reigns of Amaziah of Judah and of Jeroboam II of Israel.

Verses 1-4: Amaziah receives an evaluation of his reign which is similar to that given his father (see 2 Kings 12:1-3). He is basically faithful to God in worship and in his covenant responsibilities, but he is not as consistently close to God as was King David. David's reign and personal faithfulness to God are the standards by which all the kings of Judah are judged by the writers of Kings.

On the *high places*, see the comments on 2 Kings 12:3.

Verses 5-6: Amaziah avenges his father's death, though under the law the men who killed Joash may not have been considered to be guilty of murder since they killed Joash in retaliation for the death of Zechariah (see 2 Chronicles 24:20-27). Joash was (in the eyes of his killers) guilty of shedding innocent blood and so deserved to die.

Nevertheless, Amaziah takes his revenge. He does not, however, kill the children (or other family members) of the men who killed his father. The writers of Kings say this is in keeping with the *law of Moses*, which is found in Deuteronomy 24:16 (see also Jeremiah 31:29-30 and Ezekiel 18:1-32 on the issue of individual responsibility). This is in contrast to such situations as in Joshua 7:24-25 and 1 Kings 21:21, 29 where the guilt and sin of one person affect a whole family. This belief in corporate or community guilt for sin is related to the commandments in Exodus 20:5 and Deuteronomy 5:9-10. (See also the discussion in "The Message of 2 Kings 8–10.")

Verse 7: Amaziah is victorious over Edomite forces and takes control of part of Edom in the Arabah region south of the Dead Sea.

Verses 8-14: Judah's victories over Edom prompt Amaziah to seek a meeting with Jehoash of Israel. Israel has been the dominant power in the relationship for some time, and perhaps Amaziah wants to test the renewed strength of Judah against his Israelite brothers. That Amaziah wants to speak with Jehoash face-to-face is not, in and of itself, a threat. Jehoash, however, takes it as such and responds with a fable that puts Amaziah in the place of the lowly thistle and Jehoash in the place of the mighty cedar and the wild beast. At least in this instance the Israelite king is confident of his power, and he advises Amaziah to leave well enough alone.

The armies of Judah and Israel meet in battle about fifteen miles west of Jerusalem. The Israelites win despite their apparently limited military resources (see 2 Kings 13:7; also 2 Chronicles 25:14-20). About two hundred yards of the wall of Jerusalem is torn down, and both Temple and palace treasures are taken. The *hostages* may be leading citizens or artisans whom Jehoash will use to serve him. They may be taken as a guarantee of no further aggression from Amaziah.

Verses 15-22: These verses give Jehoash's and Amaziah's obituary notices. Azariah, Amaziah's son (also called Uzziah), is credited with restoring the seaport of Elath on the Gulf of Aqaba to Judah. This is possible, in part, because of Amaziah's previous victories over Edom.

The Reign of Jeroboam II (14:23-29)

Though this account of Jeroboam's reign is relatively short, he reigns for forty-one years and brings Israel a new measure of stability and prosperity.

The writers of Kings condemn Jeroboam for following in the sins of the first King Jeroboam of Israel (see 1 Kings 12:25-33). They do, however, report that God chooses to use Jeroboam II to save Israel from complete destruction. After years of military and economic trouble, Israel had begun to regain some of its former power under Jeroboam's father, Jehoash. In spite of Jehoash's victories over Syria and Judah, however, Israel may have been in relatively poor circumstances at the end of Jehoash's reign (verses 26-27).

Jeroboam II is credited with restoring Israel's northern border to Hamath where it had been during Solomon's reign (see 1 Kings 8:65). The new southern border is at the Dead Sea (Sea of the Arabah). The exact meaning of the reference to Judah in verse 28 is not clear. This may reflect the fact that Damascus and Hamath were under Israelite/Judean control when Solomon was king. Jeroboam does gain control over the Syrians to the north and east of Israel, and he makes peace with Judah during the reign of King Uzziah (Azariah).

The combination of increased internal stability and greater freedom from enemies leads to economic gains as well. With Israel at peace with Judah, the major trade routes through both regions can be used to the advantage of both nations. Judah's renewed control over the port at Elath (Ezion-geber) on the Gulf of Aqaba opens sea trading routes to the south for both Judean and Israelite merchants.

All this leads to new and great prosperity for the Israelite upper classes. Archaeological finds testify to the luxury many of them enjoy during this period. The populations of Israel and Judah also grow during the reigns of Jeroboam II and Uzziah. In terms of economic and military security, both the Northern Kingdom and the Southern Kingdom are well situated.

There is a dark side to all of this, however, which is revealed in the prophetic books of Amos and Hosea. The history in Second Kings does not tell about the social and religious ills of Israelite society during the reign of Jeroboam. Amos and Hosea, who both prophesied in

Israel during the reign of Jeroboam, tell us of a society which is deeply divided between the "haves" and the "have nots," and which has virtually abandoned its covenant faith.

The lot of the common people is extremely hard, and is made worse by the dishonest practices of many businessmen and judges. Small farmers are cheated out of their land by wealthier landowners. The rich lounge in luxury while the needy are sold *for a pair of sandals* (see Amos 2:6).

Economic and social abuses are matched by religious abuses. The worship of God is either ignored in favor of pagan fertility cults (see Hosea 1–3) or is polluted with pagan practices (Amos 2:7). Apparently most Israelite priests and prophets go along with the situation, perhaps because the cultic activity with which they are involved brings them support and gifts (see Amos 4:4-5; 5:21-22; 7:10-17).

Israelite society has changed from its former nomadic, tribal way of life in which there were few class differences. In its settled, agricultural, and trading life under the monarchy, Israel has become a society in which class differences are firmly fixed and are exploited by those in power.

Covenant law (the basic terms of which are found in the Ten Commandments) has been the foundation for Israelite society from the beginning of the nation. In the time of Jeroboam II, however, the covenant receives little affirmation and covenant law is no longer the standard by which daily life is ordered. Israel's status as God's favored nation is taken for granted. Covenant promises are assumed while covenant responsibilities are ignored.

The Message of 2 Kings 11–14

In any type of Bible study, there is a need to use all of the biblical record for any given period in biblical history or for any particular biblical teaching. Different books in the Bible inform and supplement one another. Beginning with this period in Israel's history, however, it is especially important to realize that the historical books of the Old Testament do not cover all that is happening in the life of the chosen people at any one time. Certainly the writers of 1 and 2 Kings do not claim that their record of Israel's history is exhaustive.

In addition to the history in Chronicles, several prophetic books supplement our information on the years in the life of Israel covered by the books of Kings.

§ Jeremiah and Ezekiel present other points of view on the issue of corporate and individual guilt (compare 1 Kings 21:20-24 with Jeremiah 31:29-30; Ezekiel 18:1-32).

§ Hosea and Amos tell of religious and social corruption in the time of prosperity and security enjoyed by Israel during the reign of Jeroboam II.

§ Micah and Isaiah speak of the need for Judah to trust God during the trouble with Assyria.

§ Jonah tells of God's forgiveness offered to the people of Nineveh, the capital of Assyria, while Nahum celebrates the destruction of Nineveh.

§ Isaiah, Jeremiah, Ezekiel, and Micah offer messages both of punishment and of salvation for the people of Israel from the time of King Uzziah to the exile in Babylon.

We must always remember to take any one text within the context of all Scripture, and not to isolate any one message or viewpoint from the whole.

§ § § § § § §

2 Kings 15–17

Introduction to These Chapters

These chapters tell of the events leading up to the destruction of Israel by Assyria and of the final days of Israel's life as a nation. They may be outlined as follows.

Stability in Judah, Chaos in Israel (15:1-38)

Chapter 15 tells about the reigns of Azariah (Uzziah) and Jotham in Judah and about Zechariah, Shallum, Menahem, Pekahiah, and Pekah in Israel. During these years, Israel endured another series of bloody revolts in which the throne changed hands several times. This chaotic time is a prelude to Israel's destruction by Assyria in 722 B.C.

The Reign of Azariah (Uzziah) (15:1-7)

As in the case of Jeroboam II of Israel, this record of Azariah's reign does not tell how successful and prosperous his fifty-two years on the throne are. Azariah pursues his father's victories against Edom (see 2 Kings 14:7) and restores the seaport of Elath (Ezion-geber) on the Gulf of Aqaba to Judah. This port was established by Solomon and was an important part of Solomon's trading empire (see 1 Kings 9:26-28). Azariah uses Elath to open new sea trading routes to the south. The Phoenicians are perhaps involved in this operation as before, since they are still a great seafaring and trading power.

Azariah makes peace with King Jeroboam II of Israel as well. Renewed cooperation between Israel and Judah frees travel on the overland trade routes that lead from Arabia through Canaan to Phoenicia and from Egypt through Canaan to Mesopotamia. Both Azariah and Jeroboam can profit from increased trade and from fees collected from merchants for safe passage through their countries.

Archaeological finds show that local industries, such as weaving and dyeing, thrive in Judah at this time. The Negeb area in southern Judah is also more heavily settled than in years past, as part of Azariah's efforts to develop Judah's economic and agricultural resources (see also the comments on 2 Kings 14:23-29 concerning Israel at this time).

Second Chronicles 26:6-15 gives further details concerning Azariah's (Uzziah's) military accomplishments and his building projects in Jerusalem. The Chronicler attributes the king's leprosy to his pride and arrogance before God and to his attempt to perform ceremonies in the Temple that are assigned to the priests. Because of his disease, he must live in relative isolation the last years of his life. His son, Jotham, takes over administering the king's household and running the government.

The prophet Isaiah begins his ministry in Judah during the reign of Azariah (see Isaiah 1:1; 6:1). The book of Isaiah helps to fill out the picture of Azariah's reign, just as the books of Amos and Hosea tell us about the days of Jeroboam and some of his successors in Israel. Like Amos and Hosea, Isaiah attacks social injustice among God's people. Just as Judah and Israel share renewed military strength and economic gains, they also share in an ethical and religious crisis. Isaiah proclaims that the people of Judah must truly put their trust in God and lead lives that show such trust every day. Their righteousness can assure God's blessings for the people, but their unrighteousness will lead to divine punishment.

The government of Judah is more stable than that of Israel, which falls into murderous anarchy after Jeroboam's death. The religion of Judah is not as compromised by pagan practices as that of Israel. Nevertheless, Judah is not as well off spiritually as she is economically, because the high places of pagan worship are still in use. Spiritual poverty and lack of faithfulness to the covenant are to be the downfall of both Judah and Israel. Beginning in this age, the voices of the prophets are raised more and more in protest against the unfaithfulness of the people and of their leaders. The kings of both the north and the south increasingly ignore the fact that it is the covenant relationship with God that made the Israelites a people and that sustains their existence.

The Reign of Zechariah (15:8-12)

Zechariah is the last member of the house of Jehu to reign in Israel (see verse 12; 2 Kings 10:30). His assassination also marks the beginning of more than a decade of violence and near anarchy in the government of Israel. In the last twenty-three years of Israel's existence, the nation has six kings, five of whom gain the throne by murder.

Around the time of Zechariah's death, King Tiglath-pileser III comes to the throne of Assyria. He begins an aggressive policy of expansion and conquest that will eventually make Assyria the dominant power in the ancient Near East. Our knowledge of this period through the fall of Israel in 722 B.C. comes from extensive records left by Assyrian kings as well as from the biblical books of Kings, Chronicles, Isaiah, Hosea, and Micah.

The Reign of Shallum (15:13-16)

After murdering Zechariah, Shallum lasts only one month on the throne. He is killed by Menahem, who is perhaps from the tribe of Manasseh and whose base of power is in Tirzah, a former capital of Israel.

Menahem displays a brutality unusual even for the bloodthirsty state of affairs in Israel. Tappuah is a town on the border between the territories of Ephraim and Manasseh, and its residents may support an Ephraimite for the throne instead of Menahem. The new king uses the same cruel methods used by the Assyrians in order to establish his hold on the land.

The Reign of Menahem (15:17-22)

Menahem remains on the throne for ten years, during which time Israel loses its independence and becomes a vassal state of Assyria. King Tiglath-pileser (here called *Pul*, his Babylonian name) has begun military campaigns toward the west that bring him to Israel around 738 B.C. He succeeds in commanding tribute not only from Israel, but also from Damascus, Tyre, Byblos, and Hamath.

Menahem pays the Assyrian king well over one million dollars for the privilege of keeping his throne under Assyrian domination. With the might of Assyria as his authority and motivator, Menahem levies a tax on the wealthy landowners of Israel. This saves the nation from destruction, but also signals the end of Israel's life as an independent nation.

The Reign of Pekahiah (15:23-26)

Pekahiah lasts only two years on the throne before he is killed by Pekah, a military officer. Pekah may be from

114

Gilead, since fifty men who *conspired* with him are from that region. The *citadel* is perhaps the residential area of the royal palace.

The writers of Kings distinguish Pekahiah's reign only by their standard comment concerning northern kings: He continues the false worship practices begun by King Jeroboam I (see 1 Kings 12:25-33). He also apparently continues to be an obedient vassal of Assyria as was his father, Menahem.

The Reign of Pekah (15:27-31)

Pekah's reign officially lasts about four years, not twenty as reported in verse 27. He and the king of Syria form an alliance in opposition to Assyria. They take action against King Jotham of Judah (verse 37), perhaps to force him to join in their efforts against Assyria. They also attack Jotham's successor, King Ahaz, to force his cooperation (2 Kings 16:5).

Because of this rebellion, Tiglath-pileser moves against Israel in 733 B.C. and captures the cities and regions of Israel listed in verse 29. According to Assyrian records, they turn the captured areas into Assyrian provinces. The territory of Israel is reduced to an area of about thirty miles by forty miles around Samaria. Many Israelites, especially those in the upper class, are deported to other parts of the empire. Other peoples under Assyrian control are then brought in to take their place.

Hoshea plots against Pekah and kills him with, as it turns out, Assyrian approval. He is then installed as the new pro-Assyrian king of Israel.

The Reign of Jotham (15:32-38)

Jotham serves as co-regent with his father during the time of Azariah's illness (see verse 5), and is on the throne of Judah for seven years after his father's death. Like Azariah, he is given credit for being faithful to God.

But on the negative side, he does not destroy the high places of pagan worship.

Jotham resists the advances of Pekah and Rezin when they try to get him to join their confederacy against the Assyrians (see the comments on verses 27-31). Ahaz will face this same threat, which he will resolve by turning to the Assyrians for help (see 16:5-9).

The *upper gate* (verse 35) is probably the Benjamin Gate in the north wall of the Temple compound.

The Reign of Ahaz (16:1-20)

Other information about Ahaz's reign can be found in 2 Chronicles 28, in Isaiah's prophecies (see Isaiah 7:1-9), and in Assyrian historical records. Some of the prophecies of Hosea (see Hosea 5:8–6:6) and Micah (see Micah 5:12-14) also relate to part of Ahaz's reign.

Verses 1-4: Ahaz is one of few Judean kings who is condemned by the writers of Kings. This is because his commitment to paganism is unusually great. He not only practices the nature and fertility religions of Canaan, he also sacrifices his son as an offering. This particular practice may be done in keeping with the ancient ritual of sacrificing the firstborn son as one who belongs to the god being worshiped. Ahaz may use this extreme measure because of the desperate military circumstances facing Judah (see also 2 Kings 3:26-27 on such a sacrifice in desperate circumstances).

Verses 5-9: Ahaz is facing aggression on two fronts, from Edom in the southeast and from Israel and Syria in the north. He appeals to the Assyrian king for help and takes the Temple and palace treasures to pay Tiglath-pileser to protect him. This is done in spite of the prophecies of Isaiah that tell Ahaz to stand firm and not give in to fear. God's word through Isaiah is that Israel and Syria will soon no longer be a threat to Judah. Ahaz ignores Isaiah, however, and puts Judah firmly under

Assyrian control (see 2 Kings 15:27-31 for the Assyrian response to the Israelite rebellion).

Verses 10-16: Judah is granted political stability and relative freedom for the time being, but only by paying a high price. In line with his own pagan habits and to honor his Assyrian lords, Ahaz places an altar like the one used in his treaty ceremony with Tiglath-pileser in the Temple in Jerusalem.

There is some disagreement among manuscripts on the wording of this text, but apparently the original bronze Temple altar is moved and the new *great altar* installed in the Temple courtyard. Regular sacrifices are to be made on the new altar, and the king will use the old altar *to inquire by* (NRSV; NIV = *for seeking guidance*). This probably refers to a ritual performed in preparation for seeking an oracle or message from God.

Verses 17-20: Ahaz has to use some of the bronze equipment from the Temple (see 1 Kings 7:23-37) to pay part of the tribute owed Assyria.

The exact meaning or function of the *covered portal for use on the sabbath* (NRSV; NIV = *Sabbath canopy*) is not known.

The Reign of Hoshea (17:1-41)

Chapter 17 tells about Israel's destruction by the Assyrians (verses 1-6) and about the resettlement of Israel with foreigners after many Israelites are deported (verses 24-41). The writers of Kings also offer explanations for and conclusions on Israel's fate (verses 7-23).

Verses 1-6: Hoshea comes to the throne of Israel under Assyrian control (see the comments on 2 Kings 15:30). Even after Shalmaneser V (727–722 B.C.) comes to power in Assyria, he supposedly remains an obedient vassal. Hoshea, however, plots with Egypt to throw off Assyrian control. When his plans fail, Hoshea apparently goes before Shalmaneser to make peace, but he is arrested.

The Assyrian army occupies all of Samaria except the capital city which holds out under siege for over two years. The city falls sometime in late summer or autumn of 722/721 B.C.

Shalmaneser dies late in 722 B.C. and his successor, Sargon II, takes credit for the victory. Assyrian records say that 27,290 Israelite citizens are sent to areas in Upper Mesopotamia and Media during Sargon's reign. These Israelites are the so-called Lost Tribes of Israel.

Verses 7-23: In these verses, the writers of Kings give their explanation for the tragedy of Israel. Verses 7-18 are particularly important because they summarize the theological viewpoint on which these writers base their history of both Israel and Judah. They believe that the real source of Israel's downfall is not political and military aggression by foreign powers, but is Israel's longstanding unfaithfulness to its covenant with God (the basic terms of which are found in the Ten Commandments).

This unfaithfulness shows itself in two major ways. First, the people worship idols and practice pagan rituals. This is in violation of the first and most fundamental commandment (see Exodus 20:3-4; Deuteronomy 5:7-8). Second, the people do not obey the statutes or laws by which the terms of the covenant are to be applied to daily life. Thus, the people have consistently failed in their relationship to God and in their relationships to one another.

God has been forgiving and patient with Israel for 200 years. From the time of Jeroboam I, who made the two golden calves, to Hoshea, the last king, Israel has had many chances to change her ways. Judah also is guilty of unfaithfulness to God (verses 19-20), though Israel is said to be the source of this sin. During these years, God sends prophets to both Israel and Judah with warnings of the consequences of unrighteousness and with instructions for righteous living. Among these prophets are Elijah, Elisha, Amos, Hosea, Isaiah, and Micah.

Because the people of Israel do not heed these warnings, they are cast out of God's sight. This means that they are no longer considered part of the community of faith and may no longer live in the Promised Land.

Verses 24-41: Samaria is organized as a province under an Assyrian governor. Settlers from Mesopotamia are brought in to occupy the land. The Assyrians use such a re-settlement policy to discourage local loyalty and, thus, local rebellion among its conquered citizens.

These settlers bring their own native customs and religions with them to Samaria. Though they learn to acknowledge and offer worship to God, they also continue to serve their old gods. In ancient times it was customary to recognize the god or goddess of a particular locality ("the god of the land") who, it was believed, had special powers in that location.

These new settlers eventually intermarry with the remaining Israelite population. Their descendants are known to us in the New Testament as the Samaritans. The writers of Kings understandably take a dim view of the Samaritans' divided religious loyalties (verses 34-40).

Verses 35-39 combine parts of Israel's covenant with God which the historians believe the Samaritans are failing to observe (taken from the requirements of Deuteronomy 5–6). Because they do not live strictly by the covenant, the Samaritans are condemned and shunned by the Jews of Judea (see, for example, Ezra 4:1-3; John 4:9).

§ § § § § § §

The Message of 2 Kings 15–17

The writers of Kings condemn national leaders in
Israel and Judah for failing to live by the covenant
relationship established between God and the people of
Israel. The covenant is also the basis for judgment of
Israel and Judah by the prophets of this time. The
prophets announce God's message of punishment to both
nations for their economic corruption, social injustice,
and religious perversion. From the perspective of the
prophets and the historians, the fruit of such sin is death.
This is not just physical death but also death as a society
and as a chosen people.

Israel "died" as a nation in 722 B.C. Judah "died" in 587
B.C. To better understand how and why this happened,
we need to understand something of the nature of sin
itself as well as the specific failures of God's people in
Israel and Judah. What does the Old Testament tell us
about the sins of Israel and Judah?

§ In broad terms, sin is personal alienation from God.

§ Sins of any kind are sins against God.

§ The covenant is part of God's revealed will.

§ The covenant and God's saving acts on Israel's behalf
are the standard against which the people are judged.

§ Covenant law governs how the people of Israel are to
live; all life is to be ordered by God's law.

§ The people of Israel and Judah are guilty of crimes
against God and against one another.

Prophecy and history alike show that God's people
must and do suffer the consequences of their sin. Second
Kings 17:15 sums up the situation: *They went after false
idols, and became false* (NRSV; NIV = *worthless*).

§ § § § § § §

2 Kings 18–20

Introduction to These Chapters

Chapters 18–20 tell about the reign of King Hezekiah of Judah. Hezekiah and Josiah (2 Kings 22–23) are the only Judean kings to receive substantial praise from the writers of Kings. Though Hezekiah's reign is not without its troubles, he, like Josiah, is a religious reformer who moves to bring his country back to a more pure worship of God.

Here is an outline of these chapters.
  I. The Beginning of Hezekiah's Reign (18:1-12)
 II. Assyria Attacks Judah (18:13-37)
III. Hezekiah and Isaiah (19:1–20:21)
     A. Jerusalem escapes destruction (19:1-37)
     B. Hezekiah's illness (20:1-11)
     C. Judah and Babylon (20:12-19)
     D. The end of Hezekiah's reign (20:20-21)

The Beginning of Hezekiah's Reign (18:1-12)

The dates given here for Hezekiah's reign do not agree with those given in other sources. Hezekiah comes to the throne of Judah in approximately 715 B.C. The books of 2 Chronicles (see 2 Chronicles 29–32), Isaiah (see Isaiah 36–39), and Micah (see Micah 1:1) also tell about his reign.

Hezekiah begins a series of reform measures to rid Judah of pagan cults, to reorganize Temple services, and to correct some of the economic and social abuses in the country. Hezekiah also destroys the bronze serpent that was made by Moses (see Numbers 21:6-9) because it had become an object of worship.

Hezekiah probably begins his rule as an obedient vassal of Assyria and paying his tribute as required. Cleansing the Temple of the Assyrian practices that had been introduced by Ahaz (see 2 Kings 16:10-16) is a step toward independence which he takes with the encouragement of Isaiah and Micah. The prophets do not, however, encourage him to openly rebel.

Hezekiah moves against the Philistines and recovers territory the Philistines took from Judah in the days of King Ahaz. Around 705 B.C. Assyria must deal with unrest in Babylon and in the west when Sargon dies and is succeeded by Sennacherib. Hezekiah and other western leaders seek to take advantage of this unrest and throw off Assyrian domination. Hezekiah apparently gets away with this for a time while Sennacherib is occupied elsewhere.

The chronology in verses 9-10 does not correlate with the fall of Samaria in 722 B.C. (see 2 Kings 17:1-6).

Assyria Attacks Judah (18:13-37)

In 701 B.C. the Assyrian army invades Judah. Outlying towns and villages to the west and southwest of Jerusalem fall to the invaders first (see Micah 1:10-15). The siege of the fortress town of Lachish during this campaign became the subject of a large Assyrian carving that is now kept in the British Museum. This carving gives a valuable picture of how the town looked in 701 B.C. and of ancient methods of siege warfare. The Assyrians used wheeled battering rams, archery towers, and catapults in their successful assault on the walls of Lachish.

Verses 14-16: Hezekiah is forced to make peace and pay a heavy fine after the Assyrian successes in Judah. Assyrian records later claim that Sennacherib stormed forty-six cities in Judah, took 200,000 captives, and shut Hezekiah up in Jerusalem like "a bird in a cage." Archaeological excavations at Lachish have revealed evidence of the extent of Judean casualties during the siege. A huge pit near the city was filled with the remains of 1,500 bodies, along with pig bones and other garbage which was probably thrown there by the invading army.

Verses 17-37: These verses tell of an attempt by Sennacherib to negotiate a surrender with Hezekiah. This may take place before the events of verses 14-16. Another possibility is that Hezekiah pays his fine and then has second thoughts about submitting further to Assyrian control, so that 2 Kings 18:17–19:37 may describe events after the invasions of 701 B.C.

The Assyrian officials mock Hezekiah's strategy of reliance on Egypt and his lack of military resources. They claim divine benediction in their actions against Judah (verse 25).

Hezekiah's representatives want the negotiations conducted in Aramaic, the official diplomatic language of the day, so that the common people of Jerusalem will not understand what is said. The Assyrians refuse, however, and continue speaking Hebrew. They wish to appeal directly to the people and convince the people of the advantages of cooperation with Assyria (verses 29-32). They also try to undermine the people's trust in God (verses 33-35).

Jerusalem Escapes Destruction (19:1-37)

Verses 1-7: Hezekiah seeks Isaiah's guidance in this crisis. Isaiah counsels patience and faith in God, who has a decisive hand in the situation.

Verses 8-13: Sennacherib realizes that he will soon have to deal with the king of Ethiopia, and he wants to settle things with Hezekiah. He sends Hezekiah a letter assuring the king that Jerusalem will not be saved from Assyrian hands.

Verses 14-19: Hezekiah goes to God in prayer and appeals to God to put to shame the claims of Sennacherib. He says that the people of Jerusalem depend upon no mere idol made by human hands, but on the Lord of all the earth.

Verses 20-28: Isaiah receives an answer from God to Hezekiah's prayer. This oracle is addressed to Sennacherib (see also Isaiah 10:12-19; 14:24-29). Even though the Assyrian king does not hear Isaiah's words, the act of speaking the words begins the process of carrying them out.

The oracle quotes the Assyrians' mocking words against God. These words show their arrogance (verses 23-24) and their ignorance (verse 22). These words are also the basis for the declaration of punishment that follows (verses 27-28). God makes it clear that human pride and power are no match for the Lord of history (verses 25-26).

Verses 29-31: This oracle is addressed to Hezekiah. The king is to see a sign of God's care for the people of Judah in the gradual recovery of normal agricultural life in the land. During the first two years the people will harvest grain only from seeds that fall to the ground during the previous year. In the third year the people will have the peace and security to tend their fields and harvest their crops as usual.

The promise of a *remnant* or band of survivors becomes increasingly important in Israelite faith after this time. Here the term means a group of people who will survive the catastrophes of the rebellion against Assyria. In the messages of later prophets, such as Jeremiah and Ezekiel, the remnant is the group of Israelites who survive the destruction of Judah and with whom rests the future hope of God's people.

Verses 32-34: This oracle promises that the Assyrians will not further attack or destroy Jerusalem because God is defending the city. God defends the city for the sake of

God's name and reputation among the peoples of the earth (see verse 19), and also for the sake of the promises made to David that one of his descendants will always be on the throne in Jerusalem (see 2 Samuel 7:12-16; 1 Kings 11:36).

Verses 35-37: There is no other historical confirmation of the events described in verse 35. There is a tradition that Assyrian forces suffered a defeat in Egypt because of a plague of mice that chewed their bowstrings and other leather equipment. Rats and mice can carry plague, and it is possible that bubonic plague ravaged Sennacherib's army in Judah.

Sennacherib does decide to leave Judah and is content to let Hezekiah remain his vassal. In 681 B.C. he is assassinated and his son, Esarhaddon, takes over the throne of Assyria. Judah remains under Assyrian control until the reign of King Josiah (640-609 B.C.). The Assyrian empire lasts until 612 B.C. when Nineveh, the capital of Assyria, is destroyed by the Babylonians.

Hezekiah's Illness (20:1-11)

Hezekiah's illness probably comes before the Assyrian attacks on Judah in 701 B.C., when Merodach-baladan is still in power in Babylon (see verse 12). The king prays for God to remember his goodness and faithfulness which, it is implied, should be grounds for God to heal him.

God does respond through Isaiah with a prophecy of healing (verses 5-6) and a sign of its fulfillment (verses 8-11). The prophecy, however, is about Jerusalem as well as about Hezekiah. The king's well-being is tied to that of the city. God promises Hezekiah that Jerusalem will be saved, not on his own merit or that of the people, but for the sake of God's chosen city and God's chosen rulers (see also 2 Kings 19:34).

Figs are commonly used as a poultice on ulcers and boils.

Judah and Babylon (20:12-21)

The Babylonian ruler sends his envoys to make a courtesy call on Hezekiah and also to enlist Judean support in Babylon's rebellion against Assyria. Hezekiah's great show of hospitality to these visitors indicates to Isaiah that the king will indeed join the rebellion. This is the reason Isaiah reacts so strongly to the king showing the Babylonians the riches and weapons at his disposal.

During the reign of Ahaz, Isaiah had advised the king not to seek Assyrian help too quickly (see Isaiah 7:1-17). Once Judah allies with Assyria, however, Isaiah warns Hezekiah not to rebel (see Isaiah 7:17; 20:1-6) but to submit to Assyria as part of God's will for Judah (see also 2 Chronicles 32:31). In this way the stability and leadership of the nation can be preserved until a time when Judah will not be faced with such an overwhelming foe.

The prophetic oracle in verses 16-18 is to be seen in the context of Hezekiah's plans for rebellion against Assyria. Isaiah rebukes the king for his intentions to rebel and tells him that, in the future, it is Babylon and not Assyria that will devastate Judah. Isaiah tries to get Hezekiah to see that God is Judah's only dependable, long-term ally.

In verse 18, *your sons* (NRSV) means *your descendants* (NIV).

Hezekiah responds that the news is reliable (*good*), though not favorable. He accepts the announcement of punishment but is grateful that it is for a future time.

The End of Hezekiah's Reign (20:20-21)

Among Hezekiah's preparations for military conflict in Jerusalem is the construction of the Siloam tunnel (sometimes called Hezekiah's tunnel; see also 2 Chronicles 32:30; Isaiah 22:8b-11). This tunnel runs from a spring outside the city walls through 1,700 feet of rock to a pool inside the city. This insures Jerusalem an adequate supply of water during a siege.

Second Chronicles 32:32-33 gives further details about the records of Hezekiah's reign and about his funeral.

§ § § § § § §

The Message of 2 Kings 18–20

The biblical record shows that God uses other peoples as tools of punishment against the people of Israel when God's chosen people have been disobedient to the covenant relationship. For example, God uses Syria (see 2 Kings 8:10-13), Assyria (see Amos 3:9-11), and Babylon (see Jeremiah 21:1-10). These tools of punishment, however, are not themselves above judgment (see, for example, Nahum 1:15; 3:18-19; Jeremiah 50:29-30).

Prophetic announcements of punishment and God's actions against Israel and against other nations are all related to particular historical circumstances. In each case there is a crisis of faith and of faithfulness to the covenant in the life of the people of Israel. These texts show how the people of Israel and other peoples of the earth are in relationship with God, though they may not always be aware of this relationship.

What do these texts tell us about God's relationship to the peoples of the earth?

§ God is the Lord of all peoples.

§ God rules the affairs of all humankind.

§ Human pride and strength always give way before God's strength.

§ God's will is revealed to the people of Israel, in part, through the words of the prophets.

§ The word of God spoken by the prophets affects not only Israel but other nations as well.

§ The people of Israel must choose to obey God and live or disobey and die.

§ God's long-term will for human history is for a loving and redeeming relationship with all peoples.

§ § § § § § §

2 Kings 21–23

Introduction to These Chapters

Second Kings 21–23 covers the reigns of Manasseh,
Amon, and Josiah. The writers of Kings emphasize the
contrast between the religious policies of Manasseh and
Amon on the one hand, and Josiah on the other.
Manasseh and Amon are condemned as the worst kings
ever to reign in Judah. Josiah is praised as the most
faithful king.

Biblical sources for this time in the history of Judah are
2 Kings 21–23; 2 Chronicles 33–35; Jeremiah 1–6; Nahum;
Habakkuk; and Zephaniah. Assyrian and Babylonian
records also provide information about these countries'
dealings with Judah.

Here is an outline of 2 Kings 21–23.
  I. The Reign of Manasseh (21:1-18)
 II. The Reign of Amon (21:19-26)
III. The Reign of Josiah (22:1–23:30)
      A. The book of the law is found (22:1-20)
      B. Josiah's religious reform (23:1-30)
 IV. The reign of Jehoahaz (23:31-37)

The Reign of Manasseh (21:1-18)

The history of Manasseh's reign in 2 Kings focuses on
his religious activities and ignores his other activities,
such as his relationship with Assyria. Assyrian
documents testify that he is a loyal vassal who pays
heavy tribute to them and who supports their military

operations against Egypt. In exchange for his cooperation, Manasseh is granted some privileges by his Assyrian overlords.

In reality, Manasseh has little choice but to submit to Assyrian domination. The Assyrian empire reaches its greatest strength during this time, and any attempt to establish Judah's independence would be cruelly crushed. Second Chronicles 33:11-13 tells of Manasseh being taken as a captive to Babylon by the Assyrians. This is perhaps in relation to an uprising against Assyria in 652-648 B.C., in which Manasseh may have participated to some extent. The Assyrians are lenient with him, however, and he is allowed to return home, though archaeological evidence indicates that Assyrian captains are stationed in Judah at this time.

Second Chronicles 33:14 says that Manasseh strengthens the fortifications of Jerusalem and sends some of his own army captains to other fortified cities in Judah. The Assyrians perhaps allow him to do this in order to have a loyal, fortified vassal state between them and the Egyptians who consistently cause trouble for them.

The picture of Manasseh in 2 Kings is one of unrelenting sin. The material in 2 Chronicles 33:14-17 gives another perspective on his reign. In addition to strengthening Judah's military position, Manasseh gets rid of some of the blatantly pagan practices in Israelite worship. He sends priests out to local shrines and high places where the people are allowed to continue sacrifices. They now sacrifice to God rather than to idols. To the historians of Kings, however, such reform does not go far enough. They view any worship and sacrifice outside of the Jerusalem Temple as impure and tainted with pagan practices. Thus they condemn any worship in local shrines or on high places even though such worship may be directed to God.

Verses 1-9: Manasseh reigns approximately forty-five

years rather than fifty-five. He brings back the Canaanite and Phoenician cult practices done away with by his father, Hezekiah, and adds even more.

The *host of heaven* (NRSV; NIV = *starry hosts*) are perhaps members of the heavenly court, or are the stars and planets themselves. Worship of the heavens is practiced both by the Assyrians and by other neighboring peoples.

Human sacrifice is forbidden in Israelite law as is the practice of magical arts (see Deuteronomy 18:9-12). Trying to read the future by magic or to contact ghosts and spirits is a vexation to God.

Manasseh defiles the Temple by putting the image of the goddess Asherah there. This will cause God to withdraw the divine presence (symbolized by God's *name*) from the Temple. The writers of Kings know also that such unfaithfulness to the covenant will lead to Israel's exile from the Promised Land (see Deuteronomy 12:5, 29-31; 18:9-14; 1 Kings 2:1-4; Jeremiah 7).

Verses 10-18: Unnamed prophets declare God's word concerning Manasseh's sins and those of the people he seduces into doing evil. The *measuring line* and the *plummet* (or *plumb line*) are surveying tools that symbolize the destruction God brought on Samaria and on the house of Ahab. God is planning the same fate for Judah, because Judah is following in the unfaithful footsteps of Israel.

Manasseh persecutes those who are loyal to God and who protest his pagan activities. The contamination of Israelite worship brings about a weakening of covenant law. Social injustice and violence are all too real in Judah, and, despite the reforms spoken of in 2 Chronicles 33, these abuses continue into the reign of Josiah (see, for example, Zephaniah 1:1-9; 3:1-7).

Despite the fact that Manasseh has a long reign and successfully gets Judah through these years without bringing the wrath of the Assyrians down on the country, his memory is not honored by the historians of Kings. That he failed in religious matters is more important to them than anything else.

The Reign of Amon (21:19-26)

Amon lasts only two years on the throne before he is assassinated by some of his *servants* (perhaps court officials). The writers of Kings give the impression that Amon is killed because he continues the idol worship fostered in Judah by his father. The political situation at the time, however, probably has as much to do with his death as does idolatry; perhaps more.

Amon apparently also continues to be a loyal subject of Assyria, as his father had been. There are people who want to gain independence for Judah and who want to throw off Assyrian domination. They are probably encouraged to take action against Amon and, thus, against Assyria, by the fact that the Assyrian empire is beginning to weaken about this time and Egypt is gaining new strength.

Egypt has traditionally encouraged the people of Israel in any rebellion against eastern powers in order to extend its own influence into Palestine.

The *people of the land* are probably a group of the more powerful landowners. They react to Amon's death by killing the assassins and avenging the king's murder. They also keep the throne of Judah in the line of David by acclaiming Amon's young son, Josiah, as king. This holds off any Assyrian retaliation and maintains the traditional stability and hope for the future that is associated with the dynasty of David.

Amon is buried in the garden of the palace, perhaps because the area set aside for the tombs of the kings has become overcrowded.

The Reign of Josiah (22:1–23:30)

King Josiah's reign is celebrated as one of the most faithful in all of Judah's history. As in the case of the earlier kings Manasseh and Amon, the writers of Kings focus on Josiah's religious activities and leave out information concerning his political policies. As is nearly always the case, however, politics and religion are inseparable in Judah.

Little is known about Josiah's early years on the throne, but he probably has advisors among the group of people who supported his succession to the throne after his father's death. During these years Judah apparently is a quiet vassal of Assyria, but is also waiting for the proper time to assert her independence. By Josiah's twelfth year as king (629/628 B.C.), Assyria's hold on her western subjects has loosened enough that Josiah can begin the process of rebellion by getting rid of pagan cults (including those of Assyria) which are practiced in Judah (see 2 Chronicles 34:3-7).

Josiah also ventures into provinces in Samaria which are outside of his official control to rid the land of pagan worship centers.

Josiah launches a full-scale reform of Israelite worship, which includes making repairs on the Temple and cleansing it of all pagan abominations. The books of 2 Kings and 2 Chronicles do not completely agree on the time or the sequence of these reform efforts. Apparently, however, Josiah begins the reform as part of his efforts toward independence as well as for religious reasons. In the course of making repairs on the Temple, a *book of the law* is found that profoundly affects the whole reform program. The content of this book intensifies Josiah's efforts and encourages the people to thoroughly renew the true worship of God and to seek their independence.

The Book of the Law Is Found (22:1-20)

Verses 1-10: Josiah orders that money collected in the Temple be used to pay for Temple repairs (see also 2 Kings 12:4-16 on a similar situation in the reign of Jehoash).

The book of the law is a copy of the book of Deuteronomy which has been misplaced and, apparently, forgotten for some time.

Verses 11-20: Josiah is distressed when he hears the words of the book because he knows how disobedient the people of Judah have been regarding these laws (see, for example, Deuteronomy 6:13-15).

The king sends his officials to seek a word from God through Huldah the prophetess, just as other kings consulted with prophets about major issues facing them (see 1 Kings 22:5; 2 Kings 19:1-11). Huldah announces God's judgment on Judah because the people have forsaken God in favor of idols (see also 2 Kings 21:10-15). Josiah's humility and grief over the sins of his people will be rewarded because he will not live to see the coming desolation.

Josiah's Religious Reform (23:1-30)

The copy of Deuteronomy that guides Josiah's further reform efforts contains ancient laws that come from the legal traditions of Israel's earliest times. The strictness of the requirements concerning faithfulness and fidelity to God are in sharp contrast to the accommodations that have been made in Judah to paganism. Josiah realizes that the life of the people of Israel depends upon their faithfulness to their covenant with God, not just upon God's promises concerning God's presence in the Temple and the permanence of David's dynasty.

Verses 1-3: Josiah gathers the people of Jerusalem and leaders of Judah in front of the Temple. The king stands by one of the pillars at the entrance to the Temple and leads the people in renewing their covenant vows to be faithful to God. God is a witness to this ceremony which confirms the seriousness of the vows taken by the king and the people (see also Exodus 24:7-8; Jeremiah 11:1-5).

Verses 4-9: Josiah gets rid of the cult objects associated with Assyrian, Canaanite, and Phoenician worship. He *deposed* (NRSV; NIV = *did away with*) the idolatrous priests, which means that he has them killed. He ritually defiles the places of pagan worship so they will be unsuitable for future use as shrines.

The king extends these reform measures into the countryside of Judah. Both heathen shrines and local shrines to God are closed. The Israelite *priests of the high places* are allowed to come to Jerusalem and share the food of the Temple priests, but they do not serve in the Temple.

Verses 10-14: Child sacrifice had been practiced at Topheth (which means "firepit") in the Hinnom valley south of Jerusalem, in connection with rites for Molech, the Ammonite national god.

The Temple area is cleansed of objects used in the worship of the sun and of other heavenly bodies.

The *mount of corruption* (NIV; NRSV = *destruction*) is a Hebrew word play on the *mount of ointment*, meaning the Mount of Olives. Solomon built these pagan high places because of his marriages to foreign women (see 1 Kings 11:1-8).

Verses 15-20: Bethel is in northern Israel. The prophecy concerning the altar at Bethel from the days of Jeroboam I is found in 1 Kings 13:1-34. Human bones are unclean and make the pagan altars ritually unclean.

Verses 21-23: The Passover is celebrated according to the regulations of Deuteronomy 16:1-8. In the past, Passover had been celebrated in people's homes on the night of the full moon. The next day they traveled to the shrine closest to them to celebrate the feast of Unleavened Bread. Josiah's reform measures centralize all worship in the Temple at Jerusalem so that the local shrines are no longer available to the people. The people must now come to Jerusalem to celebrate Passover so they can be there the next day for the feast of Unleavened Bread.

Verses 24-27: Josiah does away with the practitioners

of magical arts and with idols people keep in their homes (*teraphim*). In verse 25 the writers of Kings give their evaluation of Josiah both as a man and as a king: There was none as faithful to God before or since. Despite Josiah's outstanding goodness, however, he is not able to wipe out the sins of the people of Judah that will bring God's punishment upon them.

Verses 28-30: In 612 B.C. Nineveh, capital of the crumbling Assyrian empire, is destroyed by Babylonia and Media. Egypt and Babylonia then confront one another over who will control the territory Assyria has lost. Egyptian troops move north to help Assyria against the Babylonians. Josiah, who is now out from under Assyrian domination, wants to keep Egypt from going to Assyria's aid.

Israelite troops under Josiah's leadership meet the Egyptian forces at Megiddo in northern Israel, and Josiah is killed (see also 2 Chronicles 35:20-24). The Chronicler attributes the death of such a good king to the fact that God opposed his entering into the conflict between Egypt and Babylon. According to this view, Josiah lost his life in an effort that was futile from the very beginning. The Babylonians decisively defeat the Egyptians at Carchemish in 605 B.C., and soon after that they extend their influence over Judah.

Josiah is deeply mourned among his people. His death no doubt leads many people to raise the same questions raised by the prophet Habakkuk earlier in Josiah's reign: Why do the righteous suffer and the wicked prosper? Habakkuk's answer is, in part, that God's justice will be confirmed and upheld even though the material evidence of this may not yet be seen.

The Reign of Jehoahaz (23:31-37)

Jehoahaz is a younger son of Josiah who apparently supports his father's anti-Egyptian policies. Pharaoh Neco takes him as a prisoner to Egypt and puts his older brother, Jehoiakim, on the throne in Judah. Jehoiakim pays the tribute demanded by Pharaoh by heavily taxing the people of Judah. Jehoiakim also builds himself a new palace by increasing taxes and using forced labor from among his subjects. Judah, thus, faces the loss of a beloved king and the loss of her independence, and also must bear the burden of the new king's extravagance.

§ § § § § § §

The Message of 2 Kings 21–23

The people of Judah are apparently not deeply committed to Josiah's reform efforts, because religious unfaithfulness and social injustice are never fully eliminated even during his lifetime (see the prophecies of Jeremiah 1–6). After his death, the people are disillusioned and increasingly disobedient to God's word (see, for example, Jeremiah 7:1–8:3). It was not enough to purify the rituals of worship and sacrifice of pagan influences and to centralize these services in the Temple to safeguard their purity.

The lack of permanent success in the reform movement illustrates the fact that faith is more than ritual. Amos (750 B.C.) and Micah (743-687 B.C.) had already proclaimed this truth to the people of Israel and of Judah (see Amos 5:21-24; Micah 6:6-8). The destruction of Israel in 722 B.C. and the coming destruction of Judah in 597 and 587 B.C. witness to the fact that the covenant relationship requires more of God's people than correct ritual. According to the prophets, what does God require?

§ Ritual is important, but it cannot take the place of a right relationship with God and with other people.

§ What is required for a righteous life is clearly shown in the covenant and law of Israel.

§ Proper worship must go hand in hand with justice and righteousness in daily life.

§ The merciful and just relationship God has with people defines the relationship that people have with one another.

§ A person's inward and outward life must be in harmony.

§ § § § § § §

PART SIXTEEN 2 Kings 24–25

Introduction to These Chapters

The history of Kings ends in approximately 560 B.C., with Judah at the mercy of the Babylonians. Jerusalem is destroyed, thousands of Judeans are exiled in Babylon, and the people who remain in the ravaged land are at odds with one another. The last four verses of 2 Kings 25 add a footnote of hope concerning Judah's future based on the improved treatment of the exiled King Jehoiachin by the Babylonians.

The books of 2 Kings, 2 Chronicles, Jeremiah, and Ezekiel deal with this time in the history of the people of Judah. Official records of the Babylonian kings, called the Babylonian Chronicles, also provide valuable information about Babylonia's dealings with Judah.

Chapters 24–25 may be outlined as follows.
  I. The Reign of Jehoiakim (24:1-7)
 II. The Reign of Jehoiachin (24:8-17)
III. The Reign of Zedekiah (24:18–25:21)
    A. Zedekiah begins his reign (24:18-20)
    B. The second siege of Jerusalem (25:1-7)
    C. The destruction of Jerusalem (25:8-21)
 IV. The Governorship of Gedaliah (25:22-26)
  V. King Jehoiachin in Exile (25:27-30)

The Reign of Jehoiakim (24:1-7)

The history of Jehoiakim's reign begins in 2 Kings 23:34 (see also 2 Chronicles 36:1-8). Jehoiakim begins his reign in 609 B.C. as a vassal of Egypt, but by 605 B.C. Egypt gives way to Babylon. Jehoiakim then must pay tribute to Nebuchadnezzar (also called Nebuchadrezzar). According to the book of Daniel, the Babylonian king also at this time takes Daniel and other Hebrew youths to Babylon to serve him (see Daniel 1:1-7).

The book of Jeremiah helps to illuminate the situation in Jerusalem during the years of Jehoiakim's reign which lead up to his rebellion against Babylon. Jeremiah's prophetic ministry begins in 627 B.C. during the reign of Josiah. Jeremiah apparently supports Josiah's reform efforts (see 2 Kings 23:4-28), though he probably has no official role in the reform program. Judging from some of Jeremiah's prophecies during Josiah's lifetime, however, the prophet becomes disillusioned with the reform effort even before Josiah's untimely death (see, for example, Jeremiah 3:6-10; 6:16-21).

The reform focused on external changes, particularly the practices of worship and ritual, while the hearts of the people still went after *worthless idols* (NIV), or as the NRSV puts it, *something that does not profit* (Jeremiah 2:11). Jeremiah has strong criticism for the priests, the guardians of the law, false prophets, and other unfaithful leaders. Despite the enthusiasm and repentance brought on by Josiah's efforts, deep and lasting changes had yet to take place in the hearts and minds of the people of Judah.

The turmoil brought by Josiah's death and Egypt's interference in Judah's internal affairs undermines what good has come from the reform. Jeremiah's voice is raised again and again against the greed and dishonesty of Jerusalem's citizens, the false leaders who promise material and spiritual well-being to the dishonest, and the people who are unashamed of their idol worship and immorality.

Jehoiakim proves to be unfaithful to God as well as unwise in his dealings with the Babylonians. The people turn their backs on their covenant faith and cling to the belief that God will never allow Jerusalem, the Temple, and the nation to be destroyed. Jeremiah acknowledges that God lent the divine presence to the Temple and gave the Promised Land to the people of Israel. He declares, however, that the people of Israel have revoked these agreements by their wickedness. It is in this atmosphere of unfaithfulness and false security that Jehoiakim looks for his chance to establish Judah's independence from Babylon.

Verses 1-2: In 601 B.C. Egypt again challenges Babylon, but neither side gains a clear victory. Nebuchadnezzar is occupied elsewhere for the next few years, and Jehoiakim decides that this is the time to withdraw tribute and make his move toward independence.

Nebuchadnezzar first responds by sending raiding parties into Judah from neighboring countries that he controls (see also Jeremiah 35:11). In December, 598 B.C., Nebuchadnezzar moves against Jerusalem in force. Jehoiakim dies at that time, either assassinated by enemies in Judah or in a military skirmish.

Verses 3-7: The writers of Kings give their evaluation of Judah's situation in verses 3-4. They relate the destruction of Judah by Babylonia to the sins of King Manasseh (see 2 Kings 21:1-18). Jeremiah, on the other hand, relates the coming destruction directly to Judah's unfaithfulness and rebellion against God during his lifetime.

Jehoiachin (also called Jeconiah and Coniah) assumes the throne of Judah with no possibility of help from Egypt or anyone else against the Babylonians.

The Reign of Jehoiachin (24:8-17)

In March, 597 B.C., Jehoiachin surrenders Jerusalem to the Babylonians. 597 B.C. is Nebuchadnezzar's eighth year as king according to the Judean dating system and his seventh year according to the Babylonian dating system (as, for example, in Jeremiah 52:28).

The royal family, court officials, artisans, soldiers, and leading citizens are deported to Babylon. Among this group of exiles is the prophet Ezekiel. He is a priest when he leaves his homeland, and is called to prophesy by God in 593 B.C. in Babylon. In contrast to Kings, the number of exiles given in Jeremiah 52:28 may include only adult males. Regardless of the exact numbers, the population of Judah is drastically reduced, being perhaps only half of the estimated 250,000 living there during the eighth century B.C. Before the surrender, many people die in the fighting and from disease and hunger. After the Babylonian victory, thousands are deported and many are executed.

Zedekiah Begins His Reign (24:18-20)

Zedekiah's years on the throne are full of political intrigue and religious failure in Judah. He is not well equipped to deal with the complex situation that faces him. On the one side are the Babylonians, whose strength the Judeans have no cause to doubt, and the prophet Jeremiah, who says that the Babylonians are God's instrument of punishment to which the people of Judah must submit. On the other side are Judean leaders who are still pro-Egyptian and who plot rebellion against Babylon. Zedekiah must also deal with the fact that Jehoiachin, though in exile, is still recognized by some people as the legitimate king of Judah.

Added to this is the fact that some leaders in Jerusalem seek to profit from the property left behind by their brothers and sisters who were taken into exile. Many people also still cling to the belief that God will never desert or destroy Jerusalem because the Temple is the residence of God's name and because the royal line of David is to always remain on the throne of Judah (see, for example, 1 Kings 8:15-20, 25-26).

Zedekiah does seek God's word through Jeremiah (see, for example, Jeremiah 21:1-7; 37:16-21), but he does not stand up to his leading nobles when they advise rebellion. In 594/593 B.C. representatives from other countries meet with Zedekiah in Jerusalem to coordinate plans for rebellion (see Jeremiah 27:3). The plot never materializes, and Zedekiah must go to Babylon to reassure Nebuchadnezzar of his loyalty (see Jeremiah 51:59).

During these years, Jeremiah in Jerusalem and Ezekiel in Babylonia condemn the idolatry, corruption, and false hopes of the Jews still in Jerusalem and those living in exile. They announce God's punishment on the people of Israel for their sins and warn that rebellion is futile (see, for example, Jeremiah 35:12-17; 37:9-10; Ezekiel 7:23-27). Jeremiah writes a letter to the exiles advising them to seek their welfare in the welfare of Babylon because it is by God's will that they are there (see Jeremiah 25:1-9).

The Second Siege of Jerusalem (25:1-7)

Despite his oaths of allegiance to Nebuchadnezzar (see 2 Chronicles 36:13; Ezekiel 17:13-14) and against Jeremiah's warnings, Zedekiah rebels against Babylon in 589/588 B.C. The Babylonians attack Jerusalem in the winter of 588 B.C., and keep the city under siege for eighteen months.

The Babylonian army probably focuses its attack on the north wall of the city because the slope leading up to this wall is not as steep as on the other sides. They also probably use strategies of attack that are typical of siege warfare at this time in history. Ditches and moats in the line of attack are filled in and ramps are built so that siege equipment can be moved close to the city walls. Wooden tracks are built for the battering rams and archery towers.

When their equipment is in place, the actual attack begins. The battering rams attack the walls and gates.

Archers and slingmen aim arrows and stones at the defenders in support of the rams. Catapults are also used to hurl stones and fire at the defenders.

For their part, the defenders shoot arrows, sling stones, pour boiling oil on the attackers, and try to disable the battering rams with chains and grapnels. They have the protection of the city walls and their shields, but the advantage lies with the attackers who have access to food and water.

The citizens of Jerusalem are near starvation by the time the Babylonians break through the walls in June of 587 B.C. (see Lamentations 4:9-10). Zedekiah tries to escape, but Babylonian forces overtake him. They take terrible revenge on him and his family before taking him in chains to Babylon where he dies (see Jeremiah 52:11).

The Destruction of Jerusalem (25:8-21)

Jerusalem and the Temple are sacked and burned. Temple treasures, including the great bronze pillars, basin, and lamp stands that were constructed for King Solomon (see 1 Kings 7:15-47) are carried to Babylon.

The religious and civil leaders named in verses 18-21 are executed by Nebuchadnezzar for their part in the rebellion. The country is left in ruins with only the *poorest of the land* (verse 12) remaining to try to put their lives back in order and feed their families.

The Governorship of Gedaliah (25:22-26)

The nation of Judah is no more. Judah is now a province of Babylonia. Gedaliah, a member of a prominent Judean family, is appointed governor under Babylonian control. He tries to restore order in the land and encourages the people to resume their normal lives (see Jeremiah 40:7-12).

Gedaliah, however, is assassinated by a zealous member of the Judean royal family who has been living in exile in Ammon (see also Jeremiah 40:13–41:18). The

Babylonians react by taking even more captives to Babylon from Judah in 582 B.C. (see Jeremiah 52:30), while some Judeans flee to Egypt taking an unwilling Jeremiah with them (see Jeremiah 42:18–43:7).

Much, if not all, of Judah's territory is incorporated by the Babylonians into the province of Samaria.

King Jehoiachin in Exile (25:27-30)

The historians of Kings add this encouraging note concerning King Jehoiachin, who is still in exile. Nebuchadnezzar dies in 562 B.C., and is succeeded by Evil-merodach. Jehoiachin is released from prison and allowed a place of honor in the king's house along with other vassal kings. He no doubt swears an oath of loyalty to the new Babylonian ruler in exchange for such considerate treatment. Archaeological excavations in Babylon have uncovered records of rations that are paid to Jehoiachin and his sons by the Babylonian government.

The presence of this note at the end of Kings indicates that the final editing was done on the book sometime after 560 B.C., perhaps around 550 B.C. Thus, the writers of this record of the people of Israel may end their history with a sign of hope for the future of their people. Though Jehoiachin is not on the throne in Judah, he is a legitimate heir in the line of David and is recognized by the Babylonians as the king of Judah. A possibility for the rejuvenation of the nation of Judah is still alive.

§ § § § § § §

The Message of 2 Kings 24–25

The writers of 1 and 2 Kings explain the changing fortunes of the people of Israel by how faithful they and their leaders are to God. The writers believe very strongly in the concept of reward and punishment: Loyalty to God brings success and disloyalty brings disaster (as, for example, in Deuteronomy 28). They testify to the workings of God in history and about the intimate relationship between God and the destiny of the chosen people. The historians of Kings have an awareness of a future for God's people in which the people will have another chance to be faithful and obedient.

We must, however, turn to the prophets of this time to find the true measure of Israel's hope for the future. Jeremiah and Ezekiel are often remembered for their messages of punishment for God's people. They also, however, speak of a time when God and God's people will live in harmony and righteousness with one another. They are able to do this because they know that Israel's covenant with God is both the basis for her punishment and the ground of her hope. God is just but also merciful. According to their prophecies, what sort of future may the people of Israel expect?

§ The exile, though long and bitter, is not permanent.

§ Atonement will have been made for Israel's sins.

§ A remnant of the people will survive destruction.

§ The people of Israel may look forward to peace, security, and fruitfulness in their homeland and to a renewed relationship with God.

§ The message of judgment is, in the long run, a message of salvation.

§ § § § § § §

Glossary of Terms

Abishag: Nurse/handmaiden who attended to King David in his old age.

Abner: The commander of the Israelite army under Saul; influential in negotiating the unification of the northern Israelite tribes with the southern Judean tribes under King David; murdered by Joab.

Absalom: Third-born son of David; tried to take over the kingship of Israel from his father.

Adonijah: Fourth son of David; his mother was Haggith (see 2 Samuel 3:4; 1 Chronicles 3:1-2); Solomon's rival for the throne of Israel.

Almug: Commonly identified as sandalwood, native to India and Sri Lanka.

Ammonites: A Semitic people living in Ammon, a territory east of the Jordan River that was controlled by Israel under King David.

Amorites: A Semitic people living in parts of Canaan and the Transjordan (the territory lying east of the Jordan River).

Aram: Land of the Arameans, a Semitic people; roughly east of the Jordan River and northeast of Palestine around into the upper Tigris-Euphrates valley.

Ark: The chest or container in which were kept the tablets of the Ten Commandments.

Asherah: (plural: Asherim, Asheroth): Name of a Canaanite fertility goddess; can also mean the idols by which she is represented.

Astarte: Greek name for the Canaanite fertility goddess, Asherah.

Baal: A Canaanite fertility god; also has local titles, such as Baal-Melqart, the god of Tyre.

Barzillai: A wealthy man from Gilead who supported David and his men during the revolution of Absalom.

Bashan: Region east and northeast of the Sea of Galilee and east of the Jordan River; well adapted to growing wheat and cattle, famous for its groves of oak trees; was taken by the Israelites from the Amorites.

Bath: A unit of liquid measure; approximately five and one-half gallons.

Bathsheba: Wife of Uriah the Hittite and then of King David; instrumental in having David declare their son, Solomon, as heir to the throne of Israel.

Beersheba: The major city in the Negeb (desert) region of greater Israel; the traditional southern limit of the Israelite nation.

Benaiah: Captain of King David's bodyguard of foreign mercenaries; later became commander of King Solomon's army.

Benjamin: Son of Jacob and brother of Joseph; the tribe of his descendants; also the territory that was allotted to his tribe.

Bethel: A town in the hills north of Jerusalem in the Northern Kingdom of Israel; an important sanctuary located there from the time of King Jeroboam.

Boaz: The name of one of the freestanding pillars at the entrance to Solomon's Temple; this name means something like *He [God] comes with power.*

Booth: A temporary shelter constructed of branches and vines, used in pastures and on battlefields; the feast of Booths is one of Israel's great annual festivals, celebrating the end of the agricultural year (September/October) and recalling Israel's wilderness pilgrimage.

Broom tree: A large shrub that grows abundantly in the

desert regions of southern Palestine and in the region of the Sinai.

Bul: Before the Exile (597-539 B.C.), the name of the eighth month in the Hebrew calendar (mid-October to mid-November).

Carmel, Mount: A prominent peak located on the coast of Palestine; this mountain was known for its beauty and fertility.

Chaldeans: Chaldea and Chaldeans are a region and a tribal group in southern Babylon; during Nebuchadnezzar's reign the term *Chaldean* came to mean the same as *Babylonian.*

Cherethites: People from an area southeast of Philistia whose ancestors probably came from Crete; served in David's army.

Cherubim: Winged creatures who are angelic and spiritual beings; their likenesses guarded the ark of the covenant in Solomon's Temple.

Cor: A unit for both dry and liquid measure; it equaled approximately 5.16 bushels or fifty-five gallons.

Covenant: A solemn promise between two partners that is sealed with an oath and/or symbolic action. The basic terms of God's covenant with Israel are found in the Ten Commandments.

Cubit: A unit for measuring length; the ordinary cubit is approximately eighteen inches, the royal cubit approximately twenty-one inches, and the long cubit approximately twenty-two inches.

Damascus: A city in Syria northeast of the Sea of Galilee; in an oasis watered by rivers and canals; an important center of commerce and religion.

Dan: The fifth son of Jacob and the tribe of his descendants; also, the northernmost city in the territory of Israel.

Edom: Land and people to the south and east of the country of Judah, named after a red rock and called the "red region."

Ekron: Northernmost of the five main cities of the Philistines; at the head of a valley leading from the coastal plain to Jerusalem.

Elders: Men who are leaders in their clan, tribe, or community; they represent and maintain the functions of the community.

Eli: The priest at the Shiloh shrine to whom Samuel was brought by his mother when he was a little boy (see 1 Samuel 1:1–2:36).

Eloth: Also called Elath; its exact location is unknown; may be a later name for Ezion-geber.

En-rogel: A spring near Jerusalem in the Kidron Valley; it marked the boundary between the territories of Benjamin and Judah; also known as "Job's well."

Ethanim: Before the Exile (597-539 B.C.) this was the name of the seventh month in the Hebrew calendar (mid-September to mid-October).

Ezion-geber: An important port city at the head of the Gulf of Aqaba; located on the northeastern end of the Red Sea.

Gadites: People of the tribe of Gad, descendants of the seventh son of Jacob.

Gath: A major Philistine city located in the region between the coastal plain of Palestine and the Shephelah.

Geba: A city six miles north-northeast of Jerusalem on the border between Israel and Judah.

Gebal: A Phoenician city north of Beirut, famous for its trade in Egyptian papyrus; its Greek name, *Byblos*, came to be associated with books made of papyrus and, thus, gave its name to the Bible.

Gibeon: Town in the territory of Benjamin six miles northwest of Jerusalem.

Gilead: Name of a territory, a tribe, and possibly a city located east of the Jordan River; famous for its medicinal balm.

Hamath: Important city in Syria; *the entrance to Hamath*, at the southern end of the territory of Hamath, is one of the traditional designations for the northern limit of Israel's territory.

Hazor: Major city ten miles north of the Sea of Galilee on a trade route from Egypt to the north and east.

Hebron: City nineteen miles south of Jerusalem where David was crowned King of Judah; capital of Judah until David became king over all Israel.

High places: Sanctuaries, either open-air or roofed, which were on high hills or on raised platforms; they were used mainly in Canaanite worship but also in some Israelite ceremonies.

Hiram: (1) King of Tyre from approximately 970 B.C. to 935 B.C.; made commercial alliances with both David and Solomon. (2) A skilled bronze worker from Tyre hired by Solomon to work on the Temple.

Hittites: Indo-European people who were a great power in Asia Minor from approximately 1650-1200 B.C.; later on their centers of power were in Hamath and northern Syria.

Hivites: One of the native populations of Canaan before the Israelite settlement; also called *Horites*.

Horeb: Means "desolate region, desert, wilderness;" is another name for Mount Sinai.

Israel: Son of Isaac and Rebekah, also called *Jacob*; the "house of Israel" or the "house of Jacob" are all the people of Israel; also the name of the Northern Kingdom after the division of greater Israel into Israel (in the north) and Judah (in the south).

Jachin: One of the freestanding pillars at the entrance to Solomon's Temple; the name means something like *God establishes*.

Jebusites: A clan living in Canaan and in control of the city of Jerusalem before it was taken by David.

Jezreel: Town at the foot of Mount Gilboa in the Valley of Jezreel, which is a broad valley separating Galilee and Samaria; a royal residence for kings of Israel.

Joab: Nephew of David and commander of David's army.

Judah: Fourth son of Jacob and Leah, also the tribe of his descendants and their territory; the name of the Southern Kingdom after the division of greater Israel into Israel and Judah.

Levi: Third son of Jacob and Leah, also the tribe of his descendants who are the priestly tribe of Israel.

Maacha: (1) Father of Achish, king of Gath; (2) Mother of King Abijam of Judah.

Mahanaim: Fortified city in Gilead that was the capital of Solomon's seventh administrative district.

Mahol: May not be a proper name or title, rather *the sons of Mahol* may mean members of an orchestral guild.

Manassites: Members of the tribe of Manasseh, descendants of the first son of Joseph.

Media: An ancient region and people in northwestern Iran, first settled in 1400-1000 B.C.

Megiddo: An important Canaanite and then Israelite city overlooking the Valley of Jezreel in northern Israel between Galilee and Samaria.

Mina: A measure of weight, approximately one and one-fourth pounds.

Mizpah: Most important of several Old Testament cities by this name, belonging to the tribe of Benjamin and located on the border between Israel and Judah northeast of Ramah.

Moab: Country east of the Dead Sea along the southern end of the Jordan River.

Naphtali: Sixth son of Jacob, also the tribe of his descendants and their territory (the highlands west of the Upper Jordan Valley and the Sea of Tiberias).

Nathan: Prophet during the reigns of David and Solomon; instrumental in having David declare Solomon his heir to the throne of Israel.

Negeb: Dry region in southern Canaan running from the Sinai Peninsula to the Dead Sea; name means *south.*

Nineveh: One of the oldest and greatest cities of Mesopotamia on the Tigris River; the capital city of the

Assyrian empire.

Ophir: Country perhaps located in southern Arabia on the coast of the Red Sea.

Pelethites: Men from Philistia who served in David's army.

Perizzites: One of the native population groups in Canaan living in the central highlands; their exact identity is unknown.

Philistines: Sea peoples who settled on the southern Mediterranean coast of Palestine in 1200 B.C.; they were fierce fighters who were often at war with Israel.

Phoenicia: Group of city-states on the Mediterranean coast in what is now Lebanon; the Phoenicians were great seafarers, explorers, and traders who thrived from approximately 1200 B.C. to 146 B.C.

Ramoth-gilead: Important fortress city in Gilead, east of the Jordan River; sometimes called Ramah.

Reubenites: Members of the tribe of Reuben, descendants of the first son of Jacob and Leah.

Samaria: Capital of the Northern Kingdom; also the name of the surrounding territory in the hill country of Palestine; conquered by Assyria in 722 B.C.

Semite: Someone who is a descendant of Shem, the son of Noah, or who speaks a Semitic language (for example, Arabs, Arameans, Assyrians, Babylonians, Canaanites, Hebrews, and Phoenicians).

Serpent's stone: Rock or stone near En-rogel; the name may come from its association with a serpent god or image; the figure of a serpent as a symbol either of evil or of healing and fertility is common on religious monuments and utensils in ancient Palestine.

Shechem: Town about forty miles north of Jerusalem; an important Israelite religious and political center.

Shekel: Approximately two-fifths of one pound.

Sheol: Land of the dead.

Shephelah: Foothill region in Judah between the Mediterranean coastal plain and the Judean highlands.

Shiloh: Major Israelite shrine eighteen miles north of Jerusalem until its destruction in 1050 B.C.

Shimei: Son of Gera, a member of the tribe of Benjamin and of the house of Saul; opposed and then supported David as king.

Shunammite: Someone from Shunem, a town in northern Israel overlooking the Valley of Jezreel.

Sidon: Ancient Phoenician seaport between Tyre and Beirut; an agricultural, fishing, and trading center famous for its purple dye which was made from the murex shell.

Succoth: City in Gad east of the Jordan River.

Talent: A weight (approximately seventy-five pounds) and an amount of money (approximately $1,500).

Tarshish: A Phoenician trading and shipping city probably located on the coast of Spain; also called *Tartessos*.

Tent of meeting: A portable sanctuary, also called the tabernacle; contained the ark, altar, and other objects used in worship.

Tibni: Exact identity unknown.

Tirzah: A town northeast of Shechem on main travel routes into the Jordan Valley; the capital of Israel before Samaria was built.

Tyre: Important Phoenician seaport in southern Phoenicia; famous for its navigators and traders.

Zadok: Priest during the reign of David; became high priest during the reign of Solomon; his descendants became the leading priestly family in Jerusalem.

Zarethan: City east of the Jordan River that was part of Solomon's fourth administrative district.

Zeruiah: Mother of Joab, Abishai, and Asahel, who were supporters of David and commanders in his army; a sister or half-sister of David.

Zion: Originally the fortified hill of pre-Israelite Jerusalem; later meant Jerusalem and the Temple mount.

Ziv: Before the Exile (597-539 B.C.), the second month in the Hebrew calendar (mid-April to mid-May).

Guide to Pronunciation

Abelbethmaacah: Ah-bel-beth-mah-ah-KAH
Abiathar: Ah-bee-AH-thar
Abijah: Ah-BEE-jah
Abijam: Ah-BEE-jam
Abishag: AB-ih-shag
Abner: AB-ner
Absalom: AB-sah-lom
Achish: Ah-KEESH
Adonijah: Ah-doh-NIGH-jah
Adoniram: Ah-doh-NIGH-ram
Ahaz: AY-haz
Ahaziah: Ah-hah-ZIGH-ah
Amasa: Ah-MAH-sah
Ammonites: AM-oh-nites
Amorites: AM-oh-rites
Aphek: AY-feck
Aramean: Air-ah-MEE-an
Asa: AY-suh
Asherim: Ash-uh-REEM
Ashtoreth: ASH-toh-reth
Astarte: Ah-STAR-tee
Athaliah: Ath-ah-LIGH-ah
Azariah: Az-ah-RIGH-ah
Baal: Bah-AHL
Baalath: Bah-ah-LAHTH
Baasha: Bah-ah-SHAH

Bahurim: Bah-hoor-EEM
Barzillai: Bar-ZIL-eye
Beersheba: Beer-SHEE-bah
Benaiah: Beh-NIGH-ah
Benhadad: Ben-hah-DAHD
Beth-horon: Beth-HOR-on
Bul: BOOL
Byblos: BIB-los
Cabul: KAY-bul
Chaldeans: Kal-DEE-ans
Chemosh: KAY-mosh
Cherethites: KER-eh-thites
Cherith: KAY-rith
Cherubim: CHER-eh-bim
Chinneroth: KIN-eh-roth
Cor: CORE
Cubit: CUE-bit
Elah: EE-lah
Eli: EE-ligh
Eliada: Eh-LIGH-ah-dah
En-rogel: En-roh-GEL
Ethanim: Eth-ah-NEEM
Evil-merodach: Ee-vil-MER-oh-dak
Ezion-geber: EH-zee-on-GAY-ber
Geba: GAY-bah
Gebal: GAY-bal
Gera: GER-ah
Gezer: GEH-zer
Gibbethon: GIB-uh-thon
Gibeon: GIB-ee-un
Gihazi: Gih-HAH-zigh
Gihon: GEE-hon
Ginath: GIH-nath
Hadad: Hah-DAHD
Hadadezer: Hah-dahd-AY-zer
Haggith: HAG-ith
Hamath: Hah-MAHTH

Hazor: HAH-tsore
Hezekiah: Hez-eh-KIGH-ah
Hezion: HEH-zee-on
Hiram: HIGH-ram
Hittites: HIT-tites
Hivites: HIH-vites
Horeb: HOR-eb
Issachar: IS-ah-kahr
Jachin: Jah-KEEN
Jebusites: JEB-you-sites
Jehoiachin: Jeh-HOY-ah-kin
Jehoiada: Jeh-HOY-ah-dah
Jehoiakim: Jeh-HOY-ah-kim
Jehoram: Jeh-HOR-am
Jehoshaphat: Jeh-HOH-shuh-fat
Jehu: JAY-hoo
Jeroboam: Jer-uh-BOH-am
Jether: JAY-ther
Jezreel: Jez-REEL
Joab: JOH-ab
Joram: JOR-am
Lachish: Lah-KEESH
Maacah: Mah-ah-KAH
Mahanaim: Mah-hah-NIGH-im
Mahol: MAY-hol
Megiddo: Meh-GID-oh
Melqart: MEL-kart
Micaiah: Mih-KIGH-ah
Mizpah: MIZ-pah
Moab: MOH-ab
Molech: MOH-lek
Naboth: NAY-both
Nadab: NAY-dab
Naphtali: Naf-TAH-lee
Nebat: NEE-bat
Nebuchadnezzar: Neh-boo-kahd-NEZ-er
Nebuzaradan: NEH-boo-ZAH-reh-dan

Nineveh: NIH-neh-veh
Omri: OHM-ree
Ophir: OH-fer
Pekahiah: Pek-ah-HIGH-ah
Pelethites: PEL-eh-thites
Philistines: FIL-is-teens
Phoenicia: Foh-NEE-shah
Ramoth-gilead: RAH-moth-GIL-ee-ad
Rehoboam: Ray-uh-BOH-am
Rezon: REH-zon
Sennacherib: Seh-NAK-eh-rib
Shalmaneser: Shal-mah-NEE-zer
Shaphat: SHAY-faht
Shechem: SHEK-em
Sheol: Sheh-OLE
Shephelah: Sheh-FAY-lah
Shimei: SHIH-migh
Shunammite: SHOO-nah-mite
Shunem: SHOO-nem
Sidon: SIGH-don
Succoth: SUH-koth
Tabrimmon: Tab-RIM-mon
Tamar: TAY-mar
Tarshish: Tar-SHEESH
Tiglath-pileser: TIG-lath-pih-LEE-zer
Tirzah: TEER-zah
Tyre: TIRE
Uzziah: Oo-ZIGH-ah
Yahweh: YAH-way
Zadok: ZAY-dock
Zarephath: ZAH-reh-fahth
Zarethan: ZAR-eh-than
Zedekiah: Zed-eh-KIGH-ah
Zeredah: ZER-eh-dah
Zeruah: Zeh-ROO-ah
Zeruiah: Zeh-roo-EYE-ah
Zimri: ZIM-ree

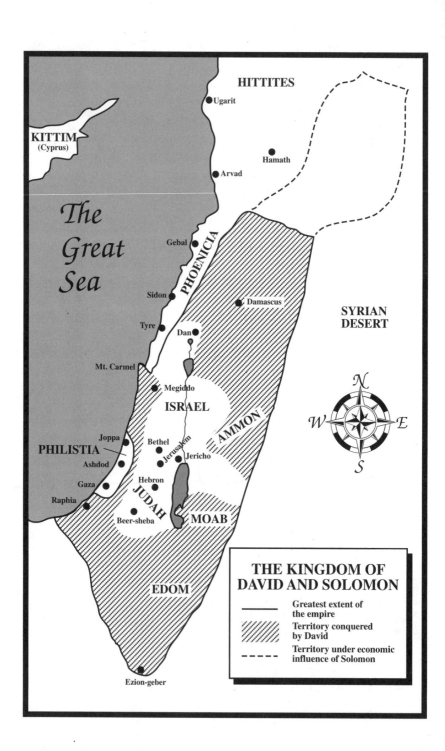

THE KINGDOM OF
DAVID AND SOLOMON

——— Greatest extent of
the empire

///// Territory conquered
by David

- - - - Territory under economic
influence of Solomon

THE
KINGDOMS
OF ISRAEL
AND JUDAH

SCALE OF MILES
0   10   20   30   40

The
Great
Sea

PHOENICIA

KINGDOM OF
DAMASCUS

Damascus

Sidon

Tyre

Dan

ISRAEL

SAMARIA

River Jordan

AMMON

Joppa

Bethel

JERUSALEM

Tokea

Moresheth

Gaza

PHILISTIA

JUDAH

Lake Asphaltitis
(Dead Sea)

Beersheba

MOAB

Arabian Desert

Kadesh-
barnea

EDOM

KINGDOM OF
EGYPT

Elath

N
W   E
S

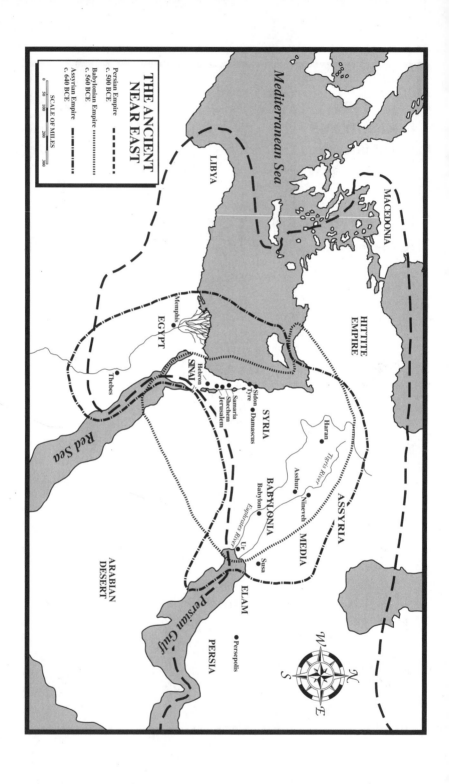

THE ANCIENT
NEAR EAST

SCALE OF MILES
0 50 100 200 300

Persian Empire
c. 500 BCE
Babylonian Empire
c. 560 BCE
Assyrian Empire
c. 640 BCE

Mediterranean Sea

LIBYA

MACEDONIA

HITTITE
EMPIRE

EGYPT

Memphis

Thebes

SINAI

Hebron

Samaria
Shechem
Jerusalem

Sidon
Tyre

Damascus

SYRIA

Haran

Tigris River

Euphrates River

Asshur

Nineveh

Babylon

BABYLONIA

Ur

MEDIA

Susa

ASSYRIA

ELAM

Red Sea

ARABIAN
DESERT

Persian Gulf

PERSIA

Persepolis

W N E S